The Best Of *Teacher's Helper*® Phonics—Level I

Our favorite reproducibles from the 1984–1997 issues
of *Teacher's Helper*® magazine

Editor in Chief
Margaret Michel

Editor
Susan Hohbach Walker

Contributing Editor
Patricia Staino

Copy Editors
Lynn Bemer Coble
Jennifer Rudisill
Debbie Shoffner
Gina Sutphin

Artists
Pam Crane
Teresa R. Davidson
Lucia Kemp Henry
Susan Hodnett
Mary Lester
Becky Saunders
Charlene Shidisky
Barry Slate

Cover Artist
Jim Counts

Typographer
Lynette Maxwell

Table Of Contents

About This Book 4

Initial Consonants 5

Final Consonants 25

Medial Consonants 45

Short Vowels 49

Long Vowels 81

Long And Short Vowels 117

Blends And Digraphs 141

About This Book

The Best Of Teacher's Helper® *Phonics—Level 1* is a collection of the best phonics-related reproducibles published in *Teacher's Helper*® from 1984 to 1997. It is designed to provide an extensive collection of phonics skills in a ready-to-use reproducible format.

Although each reproducible is designed with skill-specific programming, you may find that some pages are too difficult or too easy for your students. To adjust the skill level on a reproducible, white-out the programming and write in your own problems and new directions with a black, fine-tip marker. You may also change problems or directions by masking type with white paper and making a photocopy for duplication.

Planting Pumpkins

Name the pictures.
Color by the code.

f
yellow

r
blue

l
red

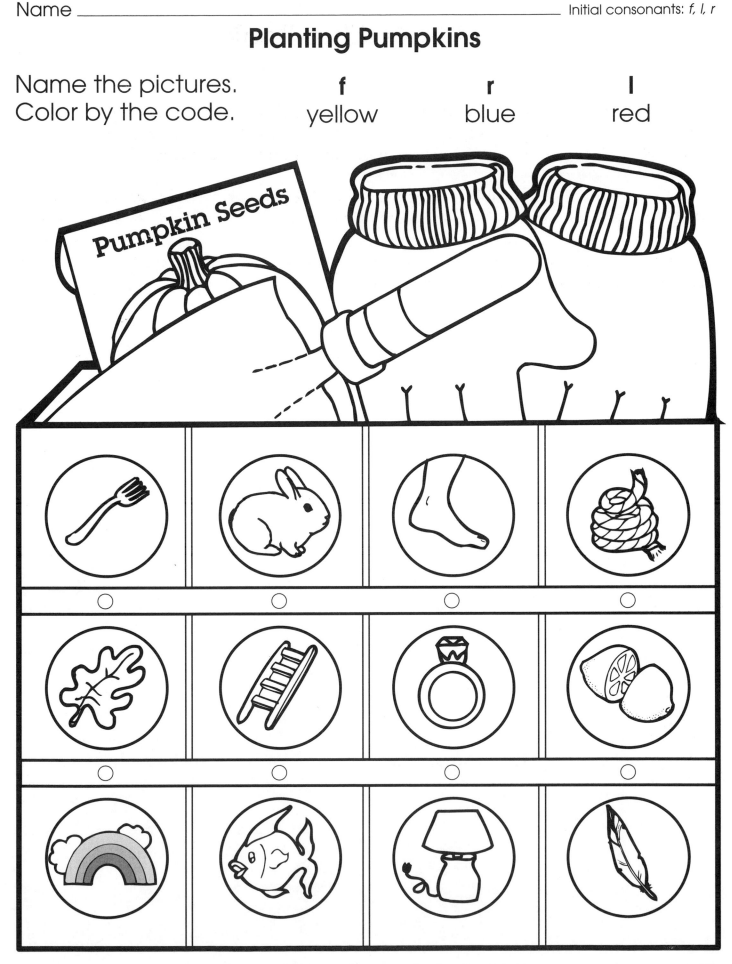

Name _____

Garden Markers

Name the pictures.
Color by the code.

w	**c**	**g**
orange	yellow	green

Super Squash

Jumbo Jack-O

Giant Grin

Power Pumpkin

7

Acorn Collection

Name the pictures.
Color by the code.

Color Code:

b = blue
r = green
s = yellow
f = brown
l = orange

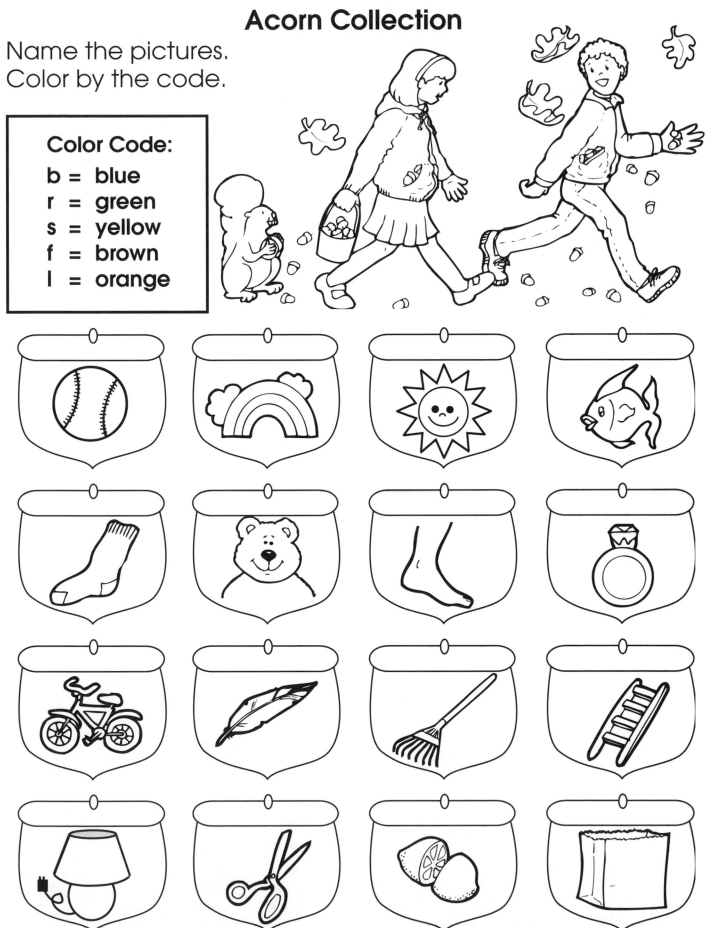

Name _____

Pumpkin Passion

Name the pictures.
Color by the code.

Color Code:

m = blue	w = red
p = orange	g = brown
c = yellow	

Football Fling

Name the pictures.
Color by the code.

Color Code:

h = blue
d = orange
t = green
z = black
q = yellow

Lost In The Leaves

Name the pictures.
Color by the code.

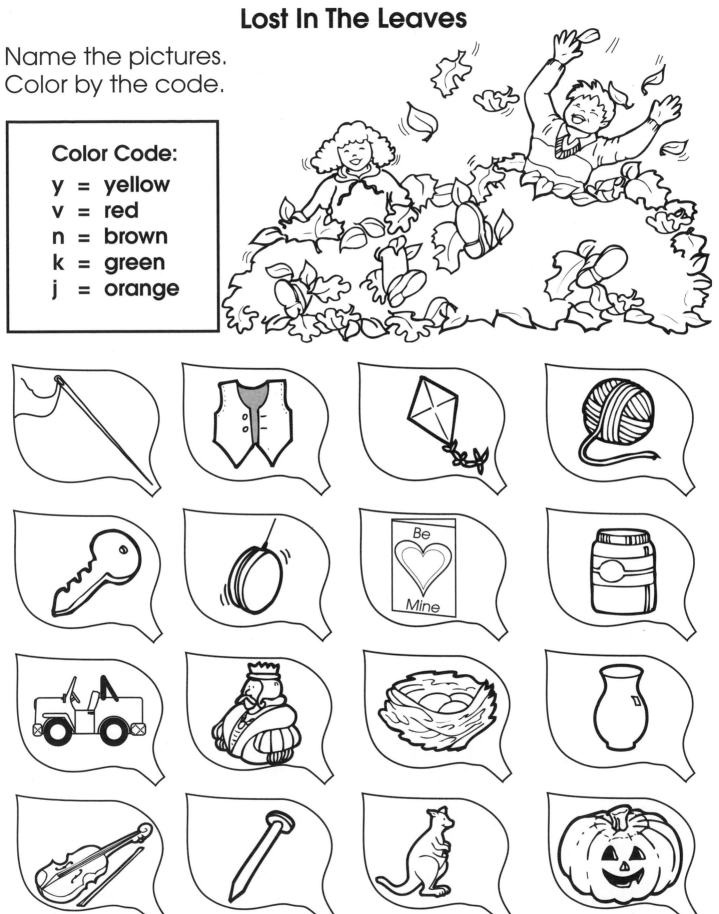

Color Code:
y = yellow
v = red
n = brown
k = green
j = orange

Rollaway Ralph

Help Ralph get his balance.

Cut out the pictures.
Say the name for each one.
Paste each picture by its beginning sound.

d			
k			
n			

Thank You, Johnny Appleseed!

People liked Johnny's trees. They wanted to say, "Thank you!"
They made a feast for Johnny.

Say the name of each food.
Write the beginning sound.

Extension Activity

Ask your youngsters to bring in clean, empty food containers such as bags, boxes, and cans. Help your youngsters sort the food containers into groups according to beginning sounds. Label one grocery bag for each beginning sound represented. Store all of the food containers together in a large laundry basket. Have your youngsters take turns sorting the food containers into the corresponding bags.

Fire-Engine Red

Draw a red line under the pictures that start with the letter.

f			
h			
c			
m			
b			
d			
l			

Background For The Teacher

Fire Prevention Week is always the week that includes October 9. It is sponsored by the National Fire Protection Association and has been recognized by presidential proclamation since 1922. The week promotes awareness of home fire safety and forest-fire prevention.

Sparky, the Fire Dog, is the mascot of the Fire Protection Association. Firemen use this friendly Dalmation to teach children and adults about fire hazards and emergency procedures.

Another fire-prevention program is promoted by Smokey the Bear of the U.S. Department of Agriculture Forest Service. Smokey was a real brown bear cub who was seriously burned in El Capitan National Forest, New Mexico. Forest rangers nursed him back to health and found a home for him at the National Zoological Park in Washington, DC. Smokey has become a popular symbol of forest-fire prevention.

Extension Activities

— Have children draw safety posters to display in the school or library.

— Invite a fireman to speak to the class about his job, or visit the neighborhood fire station.

— Discuss old and new ways of fire fighting.

— Conduct school fire drills.

— Ask children to be "fire inspectors," and have them list hazards they find.

Answer Key

Shirt Tails

Write the beginning sound under each T-shirt.
Cross out the letters you use in the box for each row.

k d r p b

n f m h g

t c s w j

Answer Key

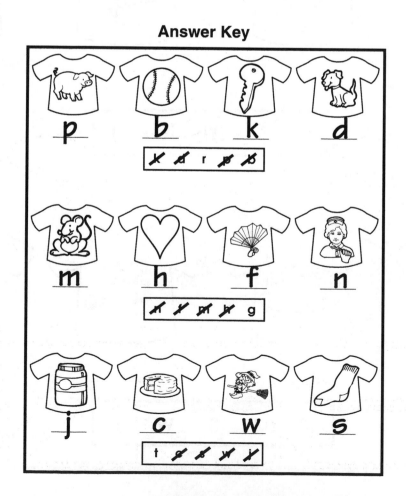

Good Luck!

Pop the balloons! Cut out the arrows and paste them on pictures by their <u>ending</u> sounds.

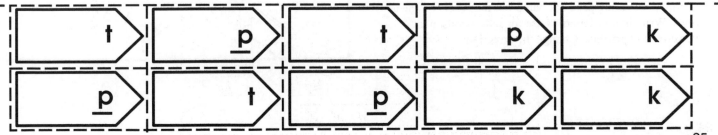

t <u>p</u> t <u>p</u> k

<u>p</u> t <u>p</u> k k

Background For The Teacher

Today toy balloons are symbols of celebration. Great clouds of balloons rise to commemorate grand openings and anniversaries of historical events. People send balloon bouquets to mark birthdays, anniversaries, births or get-well wishes. Balloons printed with catchy slogans are often used in advertising and political campaigns.

Long ago, tiny toy balloons made in the East Indies and Europe inspired the first hot-air balloon. Made from paper, these toy balloons contained a small candle that when lighted caused the balloon to rise. After viewing these balloons in Paris, two French brothers, Joseph and Etienne Montgolfier, attempted to construct a large flying balloon at their paper factory. On June 5, 1873, they successfully launched a brightly painted balloon made of linen cloths and paper by heating air inside with a roaring fire.

In the summer of 1873, a French scientist named Jacques A. C. Charles built a balloon, filled it with hydrogen gas, and sent it into the air. Soon after, the Montgolfiers, not wishing to be outdone, flew the first balloon with passengers—a sheep, rooster, and duck!

In the nineteenth century, scientists used balloons to fly higher than ever before to do research. This century has seen balloons sent into space to orbit the earth. After World War II, more balloons made of a new lightweight, strong, plastic material were launched. Today balloons often aid in scientific study of meteorology and cosmic rays. They are also used to photograph atmospheres of other planets from the clear air of the stratosphere.

Extension Activities

— Slip a little balloon over the top of a soda-pop bottle. Stand the bottle in a mixing bowl. Slowly pour hot (NOT boiling) water into the bowl. Add as much hot water as possible. Watch the balloon expand due to the warming air.
— Share colorful balloon pictures on a bulletin board to inspire creative writing.
— If there are balloonists in your area, ask them to come and speak to your class.
— Use toy balloons to create models of hot-air balloons. Cover them with tissue paper dipped in water and white glue or papier-mâché. Let dry; then pop and remove the balloons. Add string and construction-paper baskets. Decorate and hang the hot-air balloon models.
— Discuss hobbies and careers related to balloons used for racing, scientific purposes, and commercial events.
— A famous movie, *The Wizard Of Oz,* has a balloon as an important part of the story. Where does it go? Who flies in it?

Variation

Before duplicating page 25, white-out the letters on the arrows. Write in new letters to use for initial-consonant or vowel-sound practice. Change the directions.

Answer Key

Top Dog

Say the name for each picture.
Listen for the ending sound.
Color by the code.

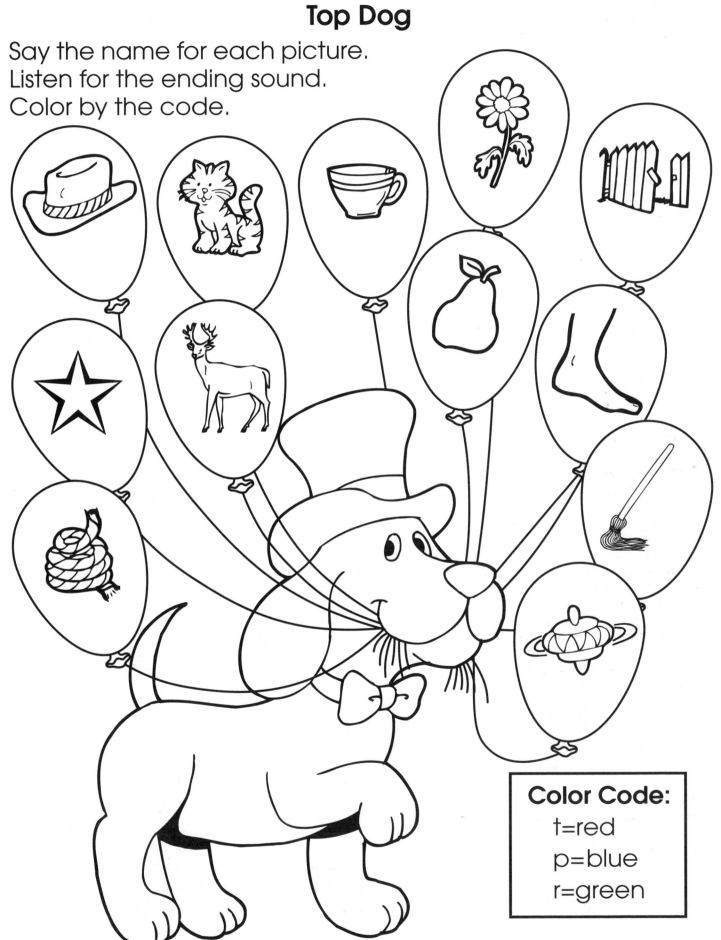

Color Code:
t=red
p=blue
r=green

Background For The Teacher

The circus has been a form of amusement since 2000 B.C. In ancient and medieval times circuses featured unusual feats, displays and animals. The American circus became popular in the nineteenth century.

Phineas Taylor Barnum opened "The Greatest Show On Earth" in 1871 in Brooklyn, New York. This showman and promoter had gained fame with his popular American Museum founded in 1842 in New York City. His exhibits included Tom Thumb and Siamese twins. In 1881, Barnum merged with his competitor, James A. Bailey, to produce the first three-ring circus in America.

Brightly painted circus trains traveled the country, bringing entertainment to small towns by rail, riverboat, or wagon. Circus workers or *roustabouts,* were very efficient at setting up and taking down the canvas Big Top. The golden age of the circus was characterized by many circus families with special skills and acts. In 1919 the biggest circuses merged to form one Ringling Brothers and Barnum and Bailey Circus.

Whenever the circus comes to town, there is a cause for excitement. Children marvel as the circus parade passes by, or wonder at the posters and advertisements. Although most circuses are held in buildings today, young and old still cheer the acts which have become circus traditions.

Extension Activities

— Take your class to the circus or a circus parade, or plan your own school circus.
— Have a Circus Day and make popcorn or candied apples.
— Have a peanut hunt.
— List favorite circus acts. Draw one for each letter of the alphabet.
— Invite a local clown to demonstrate makeup used.
— Make a circus train bulletin board. Label cars with student names or vocabulary words in alphabetical order.
— On a Big Top bulletin board, display the best work by students, room helpers, or circus learning-center activities.

Answer Key

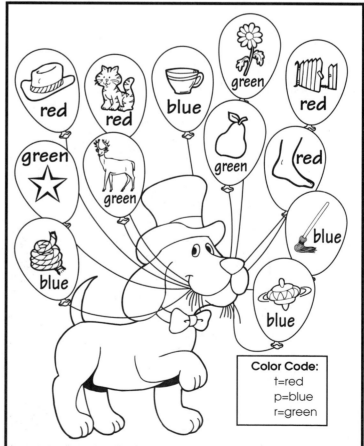

Color Code:
t=red
p=blue
r=green

The Barnyard Beauty

Say the name for each picture.
Listen for the ending sound.
Color by the code.

Color Code:
p = purple
n = green
l = blue

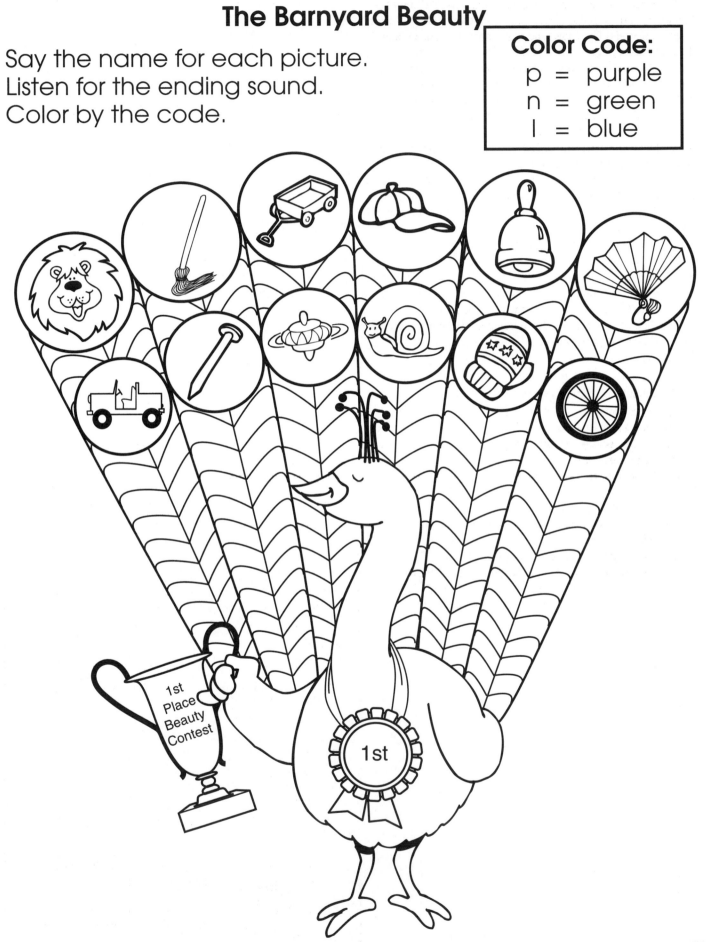

Background For The Teacher

Bird study can provide a range of topics for skill practice and classroom activities. There are more than 9,000 known species of birds. Their physical characteristics, reproductive habits, and feeding habits all differ. Conservation groups such as the National Audubon Society work to protect endangered species as well as to educate the public on scientific findings.

An ornithologist is a person who studies birds. Here are some bird facts to make your students "ornithologists":

- The barn owl's eyesight is 100 times better than a man's.
- Only male canaries sing.
- Chickens aren't known as strong flyers, but the record distance is 297 feet!
- Although bald eagles seem to be bald when seen from afar, they really do have slicked-down white feathers on their heads.
- Cockatoos have one of the longest lifespans, living to be 73 years old.
- Some carrier pigeons used in World War II were awarded medals for bravery in action.
- Ostriches are the fastest running birds in the world.
- When birds migrate, they depend on the stars and the sun to keep their bearings.

Extension Activities

— Cut out construction-paper wings that children can earn with good work.

— "Waddle like a duck, soar like an eagle." Challenge youngsters to mimic a variety of birds in a creative movement exercise!

— After children pick their favorite cartoon or TV bird personality, have them practice letter-writing skills by writing fan letters!

— Invite a representative from a local bird or wildlife group to visit and discuss activities such as Christmas bird counts, bird-watching, and banding techniques.

— Have students look up characteristics that would cause birds to be classified as birds of prey, songbirds, or waterfowl.

— Play a game of charades to act out bird-related expressions:

> *A bird in the hand is worth two in the bush.*
> *She eats like a bird.*
> *Birds of a feather flock together.*
> *Money is as scarce as hen's teeth.*

Name _____

Tommy Turtle

Say the name for each picture.
Listen for the **ending** sound.
Color each part by the code.

Color Code:
n = green
s = purple
g = red

Background For The Teacher

It's odd but true! Most people who squirm when they see lizards or snakes like turtles! Once popular pets, today neither the domestic nor the wild turtle is recommended as a pet. Turtles are being protected in two ways. In order to control the spread of salmonella, a disease fatal to turtles and life-threatening to humans, pet stores may not sell them. The removal of turtles from the wild has also been made illegal by many states to prevent extinction. Hopefully, these protective steps will maintain a link with the past; the ancestors of these shell-covered reptiles walked the earth over 200 million years ago!

- These reptiles fall into three groups: tortoises, which live only on land; sea turtles; and freshwater turtles, or terrapins.
- Fossils of sea and land turtles found in South Dakota indicate that the early creatures were 12 feet long and weighed about the same as two cars!
- The leathery plates covering its shell grow as a urtle grows.
- Female sea turtles return to where they hatched to lay eggs, sometimes swimming more than 1,400 miles!
- Although the tortoise is the slowest land reptile, some sea turtles swim over 20 miles an hour. (That's about as fast as an elephant can run!)
- Giant tortoises are the longest-living animals, sometimes living to 190 in captivity!

Extension Activities

— Bring in a turtle shell for students to examine. Talk about how the shell protects the turtle, that its backbone is part of the shell. What colors are on the shell? How do the colors help the turtle hide?

— Save walnut shell halves for students to paint. Glue on poster-board legs and heads.

— Draw a poster-board turtle with a different number of spots on each shell segment. Have students count the spots and post the correct number card on each segment.

Gone Fishing

In each row, color fish ending in the same sound as the first word.

goat

lap

fog

jar

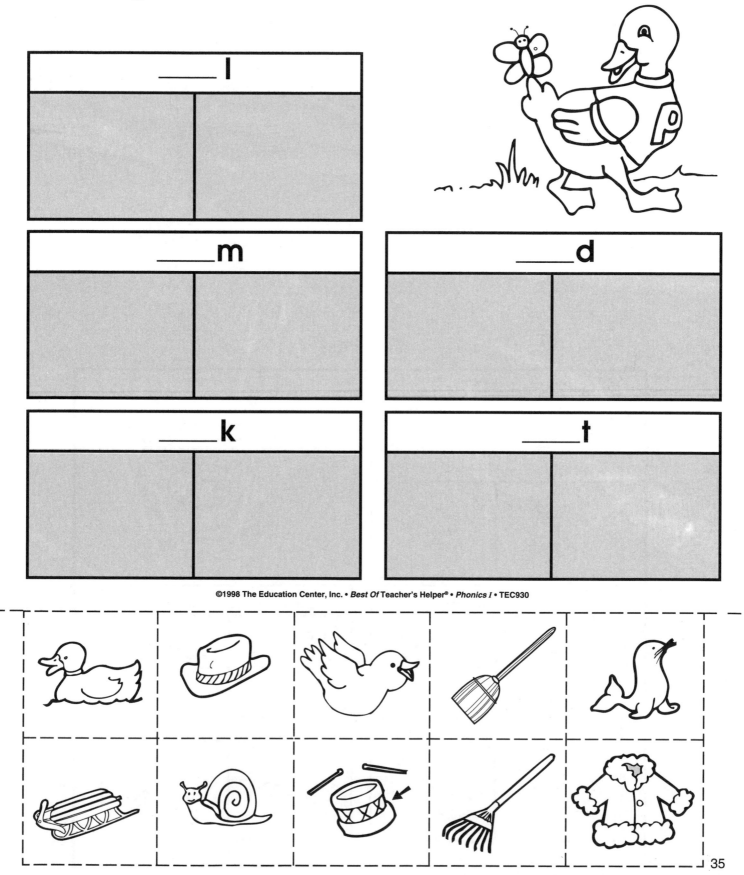

Name _____   Final consonants: *d, k, l, m, t*

Tail-End Sounds

Say the ending sounds.
Cut and glue to match.

_____ l

_____ m   _____ d

_____ k   _____ t

Answer Key

Storybook Endings

Write the ending sounds. Then color the badge.
Cut out and wear for National Children's Book Week!

Background For The Teacher

National Children's Book Week, in November, is sponsored by The Children's Book Council, Inc., to encourage reading enjoyment for children. School and public libraries offer special programs and displays to motivate children to read during this awareness week.

Extension Activities

— Have each child choose a book to read and report on during Book Week. Vary book reports by using dioramas, plays, puppet shows, mobiles, tape recordings, or video-taped skits.

— Make posters for the school halls to show favorite children's books or reasons to read.

— Start a monthly book-review newsletter for the school. Encourage students from each grade to submit book reviews for publication.

Answer Key

Name _____

Bob's Bakery

Help Bob serve his doughnuts.

Say the name for each picture below.
Write the ending sound.

do _____

ha _____

schoo _____

clow _____

lea _____

crow _____

clou _____

fla _____

gu _____

bi _____

hear _____

stam _____

Bonus Box: On the back of this page, write three sentences. Tell who gets the doughnuts Bob is frying.

Name _____

Sing A Reindeer Round!

Write the final consonant on each note.
Cross out the letter on the songbook.

Background For The Teacher

Christmas is a joyous season for Christians around the world celebrating the birth of their savior Jesus Christ. Christmas customs and traditions from many nations make this a colorful and meaningful time of the year. It is an excellent time to study countries around the world that celebrate Christmas. Compare and contrast climates and customs.

In the United States, children eagerly await the arrival of Santa Claus, who leaves presents for good children under the family Christmas tree. On Christmas Eve, December 24, in England, Father Christmas fills stockings. On December 6, Pèer Noël arrives in France, as does St. Nicholas in Holland. Russian and Greek Orthodox people celebrate Christmas on January 6.

Christmas Day in America is often spent with families opening gifts, going to church services, and feasting together. Caroling, sending Christmas cards, lighting luminaries, and enjoying Christmas pageants or parades are also traditions practiced in parts of America. Because the United States is populated by people of many ethnic backgrounds who live in varied climates, Christmas customs in America are often adapted from those of other countries.

Name _____

Restore A Final Sound

Write the ending sound.
Each time you use a letter, cross it out on the skyline.

Background For The Teacher
Statue Of Liberty Facts

— Lady Liberty's face was designed after the mother of Frederic Bartholdi, the sculptor who designed the statue.

— The statue was built entirely in France, disassembled, and shipped to the United States.

— The statue weighs 225 tons.

Name _____

Be A Bus Buddy!

Fill in the missing letters.
Cross them out on the bus as you use them.

b d f l m n p s t t v

1. Here are some good bus ru____es.

2. Don't be la____e to the bus stop.

3. Sit with a frie____d.

4. Do what the bus dri____er says.

5. Talk in a so____t voice.

6. Hold on to your pa____ers.

7. Save your food for lunchti____e.

8. Keep your arms in____ide the win____ows.

9. Leave bub____le gum at home.

10. Walk sof____ly to the door.

Cut out this badge.
Wear it so you'll
remember good bus
rules!

SCHOOL BUS

I'm a
Bus
Buddy!

SAFE

493

How To Use Page 45

Do the worksheet aloud as a class. Share possible words for those with missing consonants.

Background For The Teacher

Bus courtesy and safety rules save lives! Here's a list of guidelines. You may want to review these with your students.

1. Get to the bus stop on time. Don't rush or you will leave safety at home.
2. Stay out of the street and off the curb while waiting for the bus.
3. If you have to cross the street, make sure all cars have stopped before crossing.
4. Stand in line. Don't push.
5. Hold onto the handrail when getting on and off the bus.
6. Take your seat quickly and don't get up until the bus has come to a complete stop.
7. Keep the bus aisle clear.
8. If you have to stand, hold onto the seat. Never stand in the seats, near the emergency door, or in front of the driver.
9. Get permission from the driver to open the windows.
10. Never throw anything out of the windows, in the bus, or at the bus.
11. Be quiet. Don't shout.
12. Don't play, fight, or eat on the bus.
13. Don't do homework on the bus.
14. Keep heads, arms, and hands inside the bus.
15. When getting off, always walk about 10 to 12 feet in front of the bus.
16. If you drop anything getting on or off the bus, let the driver know before you pick it up. Never reach under a bus to pick up anything you drop.
17. Once you are off, get away from the bus.
18. Obey the bus driver.

Extension Activities

— Write rules on cut-out school buses and post for a safety bulletin board.
— Set up your own classroom "Safety Town," complete with roads, signs, policemen, and cardboard vehicles. Students act out situations to show safe and dangerous procedures.
— Invite a policeman to discuss bus rules with your class.
— Create a learning center by having students match cause-and-effect statements about bus courtesy.

Variations

— For handwriting practice, have students write some of these sentences on their own paper.
— Ask each child to choose one rule to illustrate on a poster.

Name _____

Really Big Gift!

Fill in the blanks.
Cross off each letter
as you use it.

d   t   l   n
s   m   c   m   p
p

wo____an

fa____e

no____e

win____ow

pa____er

ro____e

wa____er

ani____als

mo____ey

go____d

Background For The Teacher
Mother's Day

By presidential proclamation, Mother's Day is always the second Sunday in May. It was first observed in 1907 in Philadelphia, when Anna Jarvis suggested that her church hold a memorial service for all mothers.

On Mother's Day we remember our mothers and may show our appreciation by giving gifts of flowers, candy, or special Mother's Day greetings. Some people take Mom out to dinner or help out with household chores.

Extension Activities

— Have children cut out magazine pictures of animal mothers and their babies. Paste on folded paper to create humorous Mother's Day cards.

— Design awards for children to give to their Super Moms.

— Have students bring in snapshots of themselves as babies. Take snapshots of individual students, and place both photos side by side in a plastic pocket. Mount each pocket on construction paper and decorate with lace, ribbon, or dried, pressed flowers for a Mother's Day gift.

— Choose an easy candy recipe for children to make in class to take home to their mothers.

Background For The Teacher
Father's Day

Father's Day is always the third Sunday in June. Since the first observance in 1910, the role of fathers in child-rearing has changed. Fathers often share in child care today.

Extension Activities

— Discuss various family groups, including those with female heads of household, extended families, and adoptive or foster parents as well as the nuclear family. Have students draw or create their families in an art activity.

— Have children tell what they think would happen if they switched places with their moms or dads. What would be the most fun about being a parent? What might be the biggest headache?

— Make a list of famous fathers. Students add their fathers' names.

Answer Key

Homerun Hank

Say each picture word.
Listen for the sound of **ă.**
Color the **short a** picture words.

Hank has two things that have **ă.**
Draw each of them. Write the name of each thing.

Turtle Tidbits

Terry Turtle eats bugs.
Say the name of each picture.
Color the **ĕ** bugs.
They taste good!

How many **ĕ** bugs did Terry Turtle eat? _____

Variations

— Use these pictures also for initial consonant identification. Ask students to write the correct letter on each insect.

— Do the same thing for final consonant discrimination.

Little And Big

Trace the letters on each line.
Write **i** to finish each word.
Read each word.

Cut out the pictures.
Find 2 pictures to match each word.
Think about which is little and which is big.
Glue the pictures in place.

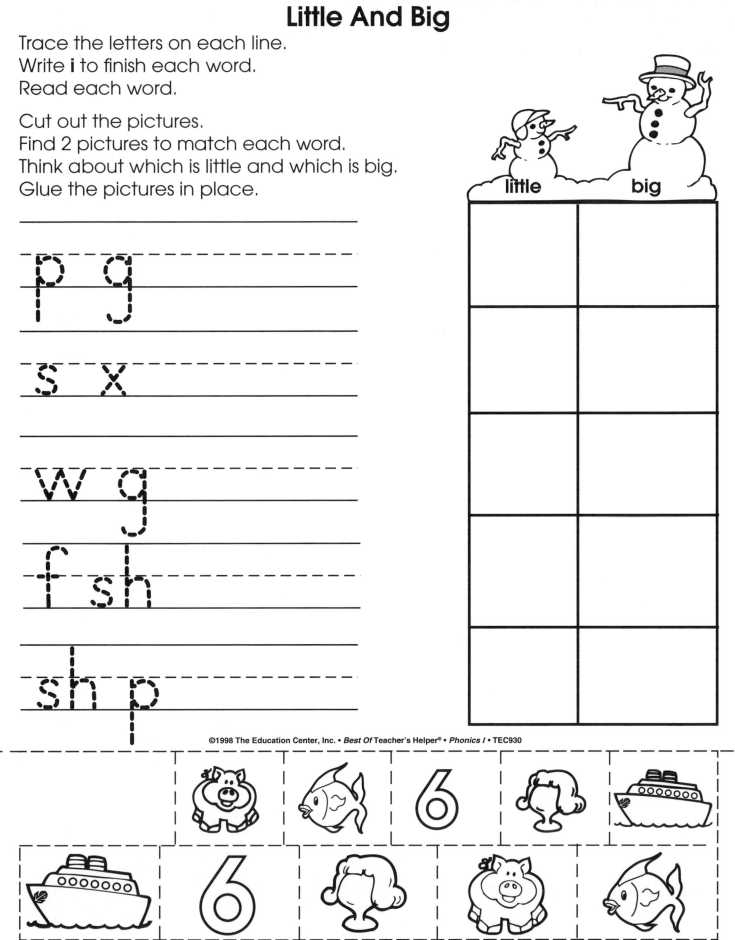

little   big

p_g

s_x

w_g

f_sh

sh_p

©1998 The Education Center, Inc. • *Best Of* Teacher's Helper® • *Phonics I* • TEC930

Name _____

On The Pond

Say each picture word.
Listen for the sound of ŏ.
Color the **short o** picture words.

Read each riddle.
Write one word to answer each riddle.
Use the pictures above to help you.

_____

It can be hot. What is it?   _____

It can wash a spot. What is it?   _____

It says, "Tick tock." What is it?   _____

Name _____

Up For Fun

Say each picture word.
Listen for the sound of ŭ.
Color the **short u** picture words.

Read each riddle.
Write one word to answer each riddle.
Use the pictures above to help you.

It says, "Quack." What is it? _____

It is up in the sky. What is it? _____

Many people ride in it. What is it? _____

Balloon Busters!

Fill in the blanks with **a**, **e**, or **i**. Then color by the code.

Now color the balloons:
short a—blue
short e—yellow
short i—red

t___nt

h___t

p___g

f___n

b___d

f___sh

b___ll

sh___p

fl___g

c___t

m___ttens

n___t

Crossing The Delaware

Fill in the blanks with **a**, **e**, or **i**.
Color the bubbles.

Color Code:
ă = red
ĕ = blue
ĭ = green

b___d

br___ck

n___st

c___t

m___lk

h___t

h___n

sh___p

b___ll

fl___g

___pple

p___g

Background For The Teacher

George Washington's birthday is observed as a legal public holiday. It is always the third Monday in February. The first president and "Father of Our Country" was born on February 22, 1732, in Westmoreland County, Virginia. He died at Mt. Vernon, Virginia, on December 14, 1799.

As a boy, Washington lived at Mt. Vernon, his father's estate. When George was eleven, his father died, and by the age of fifteen, George had become a surveyor. He became a major in the colonial militia and served in the French and Indian War.

Following the signing of the Declaration of Independence in 1776, George Washington was chosen to organize and lead the Continental Army against the British. After the American colonies gained their freedom, George Washington retired to Mt. Vernon. He was called back to public service in 1789 as the first president of the United States.

Extension Activities

— Use maps to find places named after George Washington. Help students locate these places.

— Make a cherry dessert to celebrate Washington's birthday.

— After the Revolutionary War, people suggested many titles for our country's leader such as "His Mightiness," "His Elective Majesty," and "His Elective Highness." In 1789 George Washington was made the president of the United States. Talk about characteristics of a good leader.

— Display pictures of George Washington. Have children look for his likeness on a dollar bill, a quarter, and a postage stamp.

— Invite a surveyor to bring his equipment to school and demonstrate his job to students.

Name _____

Hatbox Haunts

Cut and paste by the correct vowel sound.

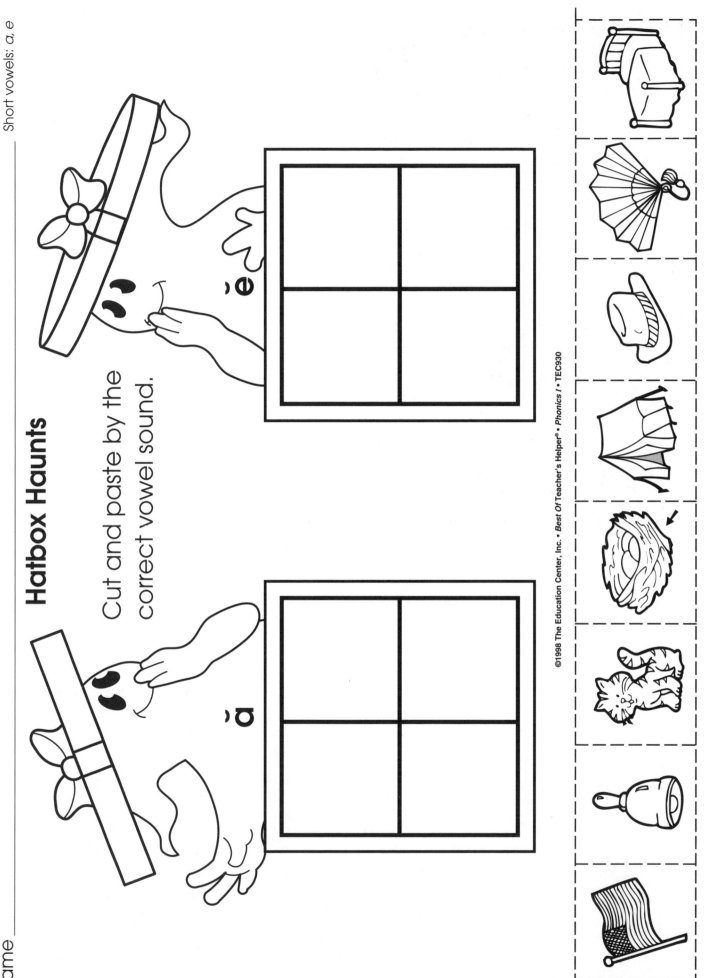

ĕ

ă

Extension Activities

— Make Halloween cards and notepaper. Provide students with ink pads, markers, and white paper. Demonstrate how to turn a thumbprint into a spooky spider, wicked witch, black cat, jack-o'-lantern, and other Halloween favorites using fine-tipped markers.

— Keep your students guessing by playing "What's Under My Hat?" Make a large, construction-paper witch's hat. Each morning place a small, commonplace object under the hat. Give clues to children. Award a Halloween sticker or pencil to the first student with the correct guess.

— For a matching center suitable for a number of skills, cut out several poster-board ghosts. Cut each ghost in half. Write an uppercase letter on one half of each ghost and the matching lowercase letter on the other half. Place cutouts in a trick-or-treat bag for students to match.

— Tape a cut-out ghost to a large, clear jar labeled "Ghostly Goodies." When a student exhibits good behavior, call out the child's name and drop a marshmallow in the jar. Keep a record of how many marshmallows are in the jar. When there is one marshmallow for each student, open the jar and enjoy!

Top-Hat Vowels

Say the name of the picture on each hat.
Does it have the **ă** or **ĭ** sound?
Write the letter in each hat band.

Bonus Box: On the back of this sheet, draw one more thing that has an **ă** sound. Also draw one thing that has an **ĭ** sound.

Variation

Use these hats for initial consonant sounds. Change the second line of the directions to "Listen for the beginning sound."

Name _____

Kite Tails

Read the sentences.
Fill in the missing short vowels.

1. The w___nd h___lps many things and people.

2. It moves gr___ss and dr___ps seeds.

3. It blows sailboats ___n b___g lakes.

4. A s___ft wind feels good on my n___ck.

5. It's f___n to r___n with a kite.

6. Wind c___n also be b___d.

7. It can kn___ck over trees and st___p signs.

8. A tornado c___n make buildings and f___nces fall.

9. A hurricane brings w___nd and th___nder.

10. Wind can h___lp, but it can also mess things ___p!

How To Use This Sheet

— Have students color and cut out the kite tails. They then fasten them to strings and attach them their own kites.

— Lead your class in a discussion of good and bad things about wind. Share unfamiliar vocabulary such as "hurricane" and "tornado."

— Make kites with children by gluing shelf paper to balsa wood strips in a frame shape.

Variation

Have children illustrate their kites with one of the things that wind does.

Background For The Teacher

Long ago, people depended on signs in nature to tell the weather. By observing the clouds, the sun and moon, and even plants and animals, they could predict the coming conditions. They realized that the weather depended largely upon the direction of the wind, the temperature of the air, and the amount of moisture in it. Modern-day meteorologists will tell you that most weather conditions are born in the troposphere, the first seven miles of atmosphere surrounding the earth. To predict the weather, they, like their predecessors, study wind, temperature, and moisture, using advanced radar equipment and sophisticated weather maps.

Although we can now predict the weather fairly accurately and well in advance, we still have little control over it. Every year weather disasters claim thousands of lives through earthquakes, tornadoes, floods, droughts, tropical storms, lightning, avalanches, landslides, and blizzards. The more we can learn about the forces of nature, the more lives we can save through early warning and preparedness.

Weather influences our disposition, health, and social behavior as well as the agricultural, commercial, and industrial activities in every region. Our present practices also influence future weather conditions. In some areas of the world, we have actually changed the climate by wasteful and thoughtless practices.

Extension Activities

— Keep a weather chart for one month with your class. Show precipitation, wind direction, temperature, and kinds of clouds.

— Visit a weather station or invite a meteorologist to school.

— Discuss any weather extremes common to your area. Talk about appropriate safety rules.

Up And Down

Name each picture.
Write the missing vowel.

h___t   n___t   s___ck   s___n

f___nce   c___n   b___g   t___p

d___g   h___ll   c___p   m___p

Hat Tree

Read the sentences.
Write the word to complete each sentence.

_____

1. The _____ is big.

hot   hat   hit

2. He is _____ .

sap   suds   sad

3. The pig has a _____ .

wig   wag   wet

4. Can you _____ the ball?

got   gut   get

5. It went in the _____ .

nut   net   not

6. I can _____ fast.

ran   run   red

7. The frog can _____ .

hip   had   hop

8. The _____ had my hat.

cat   cut   cot

Magic Hat

Name each picture.
Circle the vowel.
Color each box by the code.

Color Code:	a yellow	e orange	i green	o red	u purple

Row 1: e i u o   o e i a   o u e i   e i a
Row 2: i e u o   u a a e   i u o e
Row 3: a o i e   o u i e   a o u a

Watch Out!

Read the sentences.
Write the word to complete each sentence.

_____

1. The man _____ fast.
   rim   ran   rot

2. The man went _____ a hill.
   up   it   at

3. The fox _____ him.
   mug   gum   got

4. A pig _____ in the mud.
   bag   dug   dog

5. The dog sat on a _____ .
   bid   bad   bed

6. Is the pen in the _____ ?
   big   bag   bug

7. The mop is _____ .
   wet   win   wig

8. That pot is not _____ .
   hat   hit   hot

Answer Key

1. The man <u>ran</u> fast.
2. The man went <u>up</u> a hill.
3. The fox <u>got</u> him.
4. A pig <u>dug</u> in the mud.
5. The dog sat on a <u>bed</u>.
6. Is the pen in the <u>bag</u>?
7. The mop is <u>wet</u>.
8. That pot is not <u>hot</u>.

Good Food = Good Health

The doctor says, "To stay healthy, eat good foods!"
Fill in the missing vowel for each good food here.
Color the foods.

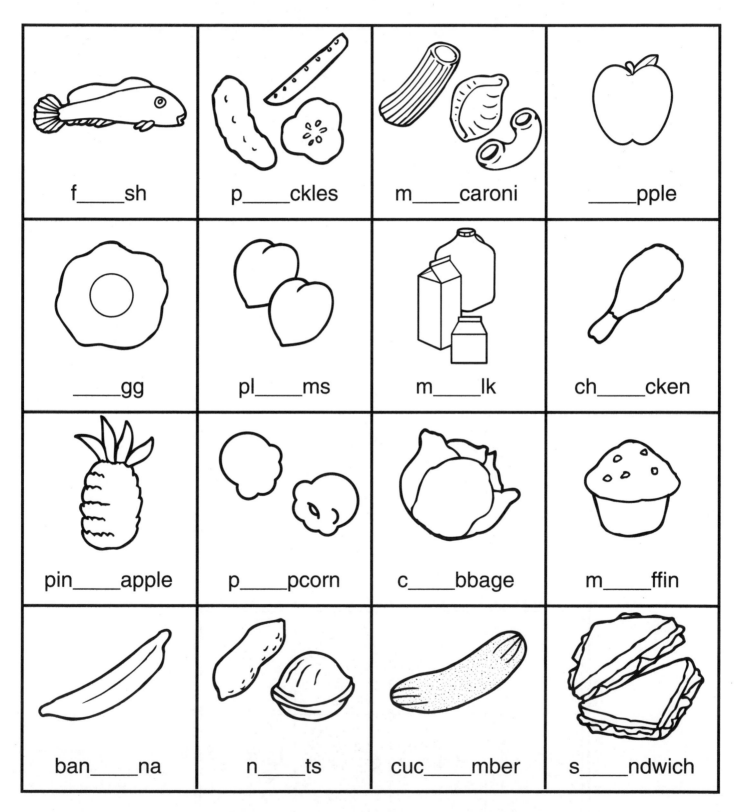

f____sh

p____ckles

m____caroni

____pple

____gg

pl____ms

m____lk

ch____cken

pin____apple

p____pcorn

c____bbage

m____ffin

ban____na

n____ts

cuc____mber

s____ndwich

Background For The Teacher

Focus on good health habits and nutritious foods throughout the school year. Observe and plan special activities for March, National Nutrition Month. In addition, plan a health study for your class on the nutrients in foods and how they help your body. Include the following information:

Protein
- Found in meat, milk products, and beans.
- Helps repair body tissues.
- Supplies energy.
- Aids in fighting infection.

Carbohydrate
- Found in sugar, fruits, and vegetables.
- Supplies energy so the body can use protein.

Fat
- Found in margarine, vegetable oils, and mayonnaise.
- Supplies energy.
- Carries vitamins.
- Helps the body use protein and carbohydrates.

Vitamin C
- Found in green leafy vegetables, potatoes, and many fruits.
- Aids in forming bones and teeth.
- Helps to heal wounds.

Vitamin A
- Found in carrots, green leafy vegetables, and some fruits.
- Important for good vision.
- Helps keep skin clear and smooth.

Iron
- Found in liver, eggs, and shellfish.
- Helps body cells change food into energy.
- Increases resistance to infection.

Extension Activities

— Make vegetable or fruit kabobs as a class using bite-sized food and toothpicks. Eat for a quick classroom snack.

— Have children decorate placemats cut into food shapes. Add matching nametags.

— Make up games about food. Using the four corners of the classroom, let each corner represent a food group. Call out a food. Have each student, in turn, go to the correct corner.

Variations

— Have students cut out pictures and glue them to paper plates to show healthful meals.

— Have children cut out and sort pictures into food groups.

Answer Key

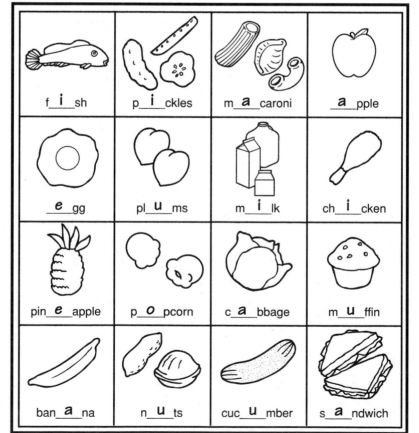

f _i_ sh	p _i_ ckles	m _a_ caroni	_a_ pple
_e_ gg	pl _u_ ms	m _i_ lk	ch _i_ cken
pin _e_ apple	p _o_ pcorn	c _a_ bbage	m _u_ ffin
ban _a_ na	n _u_ ts	cuc _u_ mber	s _a_ ndwich

Name _____

Tee Time!

Write the correct vowel in each blank.
Then color by the code.

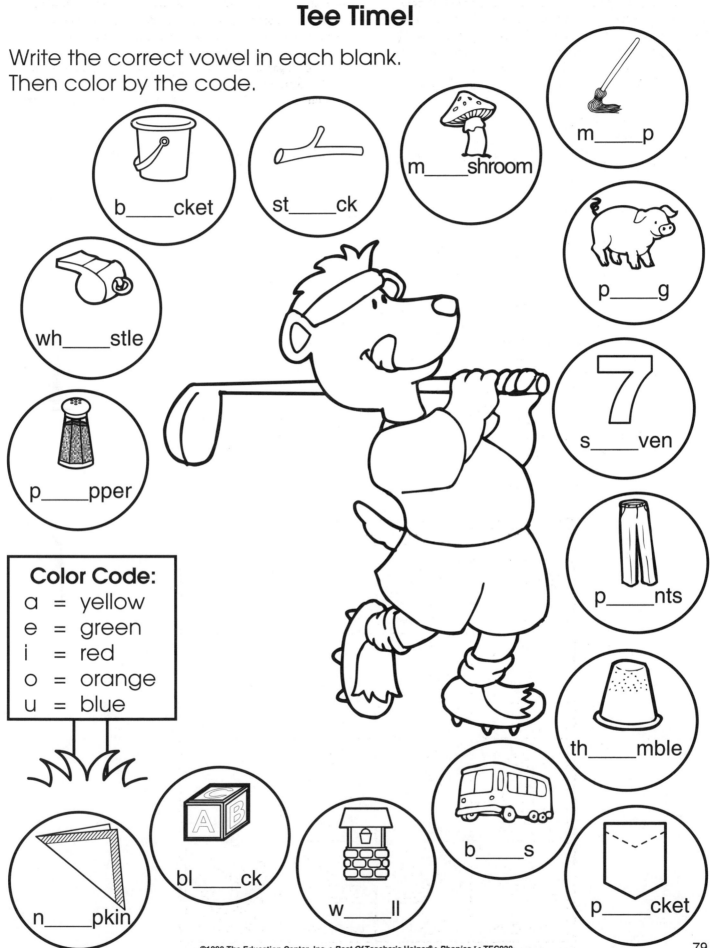

b____cket

st____ck

m____shroom

m____p

wh____stle

p____g

p____pper

7
s____ven

Color Code:
a = yellow
e = green
i = red
o = orange
u = blue

p____nts

th____mble

n____pkin

bl____ck

w____ll

b____s

p____cket

Extension Activity

To enjoy the weather, go outdoors to sample a few sports and physical fitness activities together. It will work out some of the fidgetiness, as well as open opportunities to discuss:

—the value of certain types of exercise.

—the effect of exercise on specific parts of the body.

—the benefits of establishing a physical fitness routine that can be carried through life.

—the added boost that exercise can give you when you're tired, bored, etc.

—the ways that balanced nutrition and exercise complement each other.

—proper shoes and attire for exercise.

Mother Hubbard's Place

Color the **long a** picture words.

Bonus Box: Think about Mother Hubbard's dog. It did some strange things. Choose 3 picture words above that have the **long a** sound. Write something silly the dog might do with each of these things.

How To Use Page 81
Introduce this worksheet by asking students to recall and recite the nursery rhyme about Old Mother Hubbard and her dog. Or set the mood for this activity by reading aloud one of the books mentioned below.

Related Literature
Old Mother Hubbard And Her Dog
Old Mother Hubbard And Her Wonderful Dog
Illustrated by James Marshall
Published by Farrar, Straus & Giroux, Inc.

The Comic Adventures Of Old Mother Hubbard And Her Dog
Illustrated by Tomie dePaola
Published by Harcourt Brace Jovanovich, Inc.

Nursery Rhyme Books Containing "Old Mother Hubbard"
Beatrix Potter's Nursery Rhyme Book
Illustrated by Beatrix Potter
Published by Frederick Warne

Tomie dePaola's Mother Goose
Illustrated by Tomie dePaola
Published by G. P. Putnam's Sons

James Marshall's Mother Goose
Illustrated by James Marshall
Published by Farrar, Straus & Giroux, Inc.

Over The Hills And Far Away: A Book Of Nursery Rhymes
Selected & Illustrated by Alan Marks
Published by North-South Books

Bo-Peep's Sheep

Find the sheep with the **long e** sound.
Color them.

men

bean

seed

sea

bee

nest

jeep

eat

weed

pet

Bonus:
Use the **long e**
words to write a
story telling where
Bo-Peep found
her sheep.

How To Use Page 83

Introduce this worksheet by asking students to recall and recite the nursery rhyme about Little Bo-Peep. Or set the mood for this activity by reading aloud the rhyme from one of the books mentioned below.

Related Literature
Nursery Rhyme Books Containing "Little Bo-Peep"

Tomie dePaola's Mother Goose
Illustrated by Tomie dePaola
Published by G. P. Putnam's Sons

Silly Sheep And Other Sheepish Rhymes
Selected by George Mendoza
Illustrated by Kathleen Reidy
Published by Grossett & Dunlap

Little Bo-Peep
Illustrated by Paul Galdone
Published by Clarion Books

Extension Activity

Duplicate multiple copies of the sheep cards below. Place them in a center and invite students to program each sheep with either a short *e* or a long *e* word and cut out the programmed sheep. Provide a key at the center and encourage students to visit the center, find and confirm the sheep that contain long *e* words, and use these words to write stories about sheep.

Sheep Cards

©1998 The Education Center, Inc.

©1998 The Education Center, Inc.

©1998 The Education Center, Inc.

©1998 The Education Center, Inc.

Name _____

Blackbird Pie

Color the birds holding word cards with the sound of **long i**.

kite

five

tire

mice

big

nine

hill

line

dip

pie

Bonus Box:
Use the **long i** words to write about what happened
to the birds after they flew away.

How To Use Page 85

Introduce this worksheet by asking students to recall and recite the nursery rhyme "Sing A Song Of Sixpence." Or set the mood for this activity by reading aloud the rhyme from one of the books mentioned below.

Related Literature
Nursery Rhyme Books Containing "Sing A Song Of Sixpence"

Mother Goose's Words Of Wit And Wisdom: A Book Of Months
Designs by Tedd Arnold
Published by Dial Books For Young Readers

Tomie dePaola's Mother Goose
Illustrated by Tomie dePaola
Published by G. P. Putnam's Sons

Sing A Song Of Sixpence
Illustrated by Tracey Campbell Pearson
Published by Dial Books For Young Readers

Extension Activity

Duplicate multiple copies of the bird cards below. Place them in a center and invite students to program each card with a long *i* word. While the students are programming the cards, glue a felt cutout (similar to the one shown in the illustration below) onto the rim of an aluminum pie plate. When the glue has dried, place the bird cards inside and invite students to pull a few bird cards from the pie and use their words in sentences or stories.

Bird Cards

©1998 The Education Center, Inc.

©1998 The Education Center, Inc.

©1998 The Education Center, Inc.

©1998 The Education Center, Inc.

©1998 The Education Center, Inc.

©1998 The Education Center, Inc.

A Tasty Puzzle

Say the name of each picture.
Circle the letter beside each picture
with the **long i** sound.
Write the circled letters in order in
the blanks to answer the riddle.

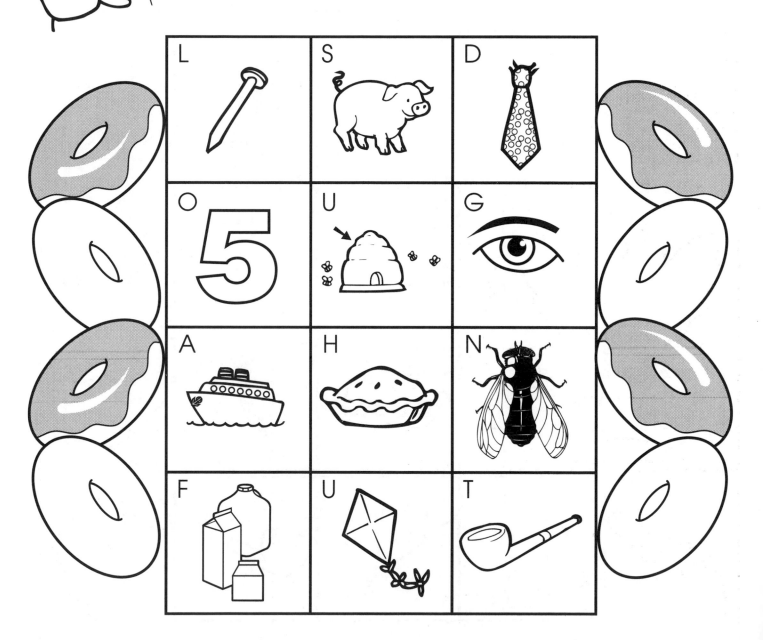

L	S	D
O	U	G
A	H	N
F	U	T

What kind of nut does not have a shell?

_____ _____ _____ _____   _____ _____ _____ _____

What kind of nut does not have a shell?

D O U G H N U T

Name_____

King Cole Calls

Color the **long o** picture words.

Bonus Box:
If you were King Cole, what **long o** things would you call for? Draw pictures of 5 things on the back of this page.

How To Use Page 89

Introduce this worksheet by asking students to recall and recite the nursery rhyme about Old King Cole. Or set the mood for this activity by reading aloud the rhyme about Old King Cole from one of the books mentioned below.

Related Literature
Nursery Rhyme Books Containing "Old King Cole"

Beatrix Potter's Nursery Rhyme Book
Illustrated by Beatrix Potter
Published by Frederick Warne

Tomie dePaola's Mother Goose
Illustrated by Tomie dePaola
Published by G. P. Putnam's Sons

James Marshall's Mother Goose
Illustrated by James Marshall
Published by Farrar, Straus & Giroux, Inc.

Long-Vowel Rewards

Get out your crown.
Put on your ring.
When it comes to
long vowels,

_____
name

rules like a king!

Get out your crown.
Put on your ring.
When it comes to
long vowels,

_____
name

rules like a king!

Name _____

A Shoe For You

Color the **long u** picture words.

Bonus: Some people's names have **long u** sounds. On the back of this paper,
write 4 names that have **long u** sounds. The names may be real names
or make-believe names.

How To Use Page 91

Introduce this worksheet by asking students to recall and recite the nursery rhyme about the old woman who lived in a shoe. Or set the mood for this activity by reading aloud the rhyme from one of the books mentioned below.

Related Literature
Nursery Rhyme Books Containing
"The Old Woman Who Lived In A Shoe"

Beatrix Potter's Nursery Rhyme Book
Illustrated by Beatrix Potter
Published by Frederick Warne

Tomie dePaola's Mother Goose
Illustrated by Tomie dePaola
Published by G. P. Putnam's Sons

Mother Goose: A Collection Of Classic Nursery Rhymes
Selected & Illustrated by Michael Hague
Published by Holt, Rinehart and Winston

Name _____

Cherry Delight

Write the missing vowel.
Then cross out the letter on the crust.

i   a
a   i
i   a
a
i   i
i

c_**a**_ke

k____te

d____me

r____ke

kn____fe

m____ce

sk____te

d____ce

pl____te

sn____ke

b____ke

Background For The Teacher

National Cherry Month is in February.

There are 10–12 species of cherries found in North America. Some are grown for decorative purposes. However, three types are mainly grown for their fruit: sweet cherries, sour or tart cherries, and dukes (a cross of sweet and sour cherries). The United States is the world's leading cherry producer, yielding an annual crop of 230,000 metric tons. Three-fourths of the U.S. crop is sour cherries. These are frozen or canned and used in sauces or pastries—especially cherry pie. In wine-making, fresh or canned sweet cherries are used.

Cherry Blossom Festivals are held each spring in San Francisco, Seattle, and Macon, Georgia. There are parades, picnics, and special programs to celebrate the event. Many people visit Washington, DC, at this time of year to see the flowering cherry blossoms near the Thomas Jefferson Memorial.

Extension Activities

— Create a bulletin-board matching activity using a paper tree and cherries. Write math problems on the tree, with corresponding answers on the cherries. Tack the cherries at the bottom of the board. Students pin the cherries beside the correct problems.

— Show several different kinds of fresh or canned cherries to your students. Compare the size, color, and taste of each type.

— Have your students imagine that they are the cherry tree that George Washington is about to chop down. How do they feel? What do they say to George? Make up a different ending for the story as a class.

Good Catch

Look at the word bank. Cross out the **short-vowel** words.
Write each word with a **long vowel** under the correct mitt.

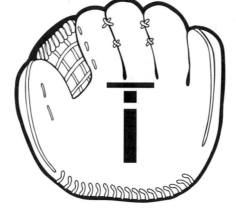
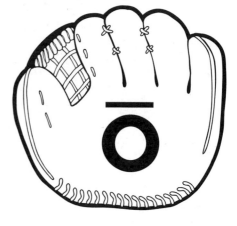

_____   _____   _____

_____   _____   _____

_____   _____   _____

_____   _____   _____

_____   _____   _____

Word Bank			
base	hit	drop	miss
ten	nose	run	play
five	game	strike	win
rope	hold	soap	line
rain	time	bat	box
catch	home	dive	plate

Background For The Teacher

Baseball teams consist of nine players: a pitcher, a catcher, four infielders, and three outfielders. Umpires judge the game plays. Players score runs by hitting the ball and running a circuit of four bases in a diamond shape. The team that scores the most runs in nine innings wins the game.

Baseball is known as America's national sport. It is also especially popular in Japan and Mexico. Abner Doubleday is often credited with creating the modern game at Cooperstown, New York, in 1839. The first organized baseball team was the New York Knickerbockers, founded in 1845.

Today there are two major baseball associations made up of the National League and American League teams. The best teams from each league play each other for the World Series championship.

Extension Activities

— Invite a baseball enthusiast to share his baseball card collection with the class.
— List teams and match logos or picture clues to team names.
— Have children match these words, written on cut-out bats, to baseball definitions written on baseball shapes:

play ball	grand slam	dugout
batter up	at bat	no-hitter
home run	choke up	ball one
strikeout	umpire	steal a base
shutout	home plate	inning

— Use team names for a baseball word search.
— Have each student design a T-shirt for his favorite team.

Answer Key

$\bar{a}$	$\bar{i}$	$\bar{o}$
base	five	rope
rain	time	nose
game	strike	hold
play	dive	home
plate	line	soap

Name _____

Paddy's Potatoes

Fill in the vowels.

Write each word on the correct potato sack.

tr___e

ch___ese

gh___st

h___se

m___sic

m___le

z___bra

___nicorn

c___mb

long u

long e

long o

Background For The Teacher

St. Patrick's Day is a patriotic as well as a religious holiday for the Irish and those of Irish descent all over the world. March 17 commemorates the death of Bishop Patrick (A.D. 385–461), the patron saint who introduced Christianity to Ireland.

At the age of 16, Patrick was captured as a slave and taken from his home in England to serve a Celtic master in Ireland. After six years, he escaped. He later returned to convert the people to Christianity. Patrick traveled among the pagan tribes, establishing Christian churches in the face of danger from Druid priests and Celtic chieftains. After his death, church authorities made Bishop Patrick a saint. Saint Patrick has been revered in Ireland for centuries.

The three-leaved shamrock originally symbolized the Holy Trinity of the Roman Catholic Church. During the years of civil war with Britain, the shamrock was worn in defiance by Irish Catholics as a symbol of their wish for independence. Today even non-Irish people enjoy sharing in the "wearing o' the green."

Ireland is known as the home of numerous fairies and leprechauns. Leprechauns are solitary elves who mend the shoes of other fairies. Usually rich and ill-tempered, they keep their pots of gold hidden and disappear quickly. Finding a green-garbed leprechaun is considered good luck.

Extension Activities

— Make a reward chart for your class. Pin shamrocks beside each child's name for good behavior or completed assignments. At the end of the week, give a surprise to the child with the most shamrocks.

— Have students cut out and decorate paper shamrocks. Hang them from the classroom ceiling.

Name _____ Long vowels: *a, i, o, u*

"Toad-ally" In Love

Write the long vowels.
Color by the code.

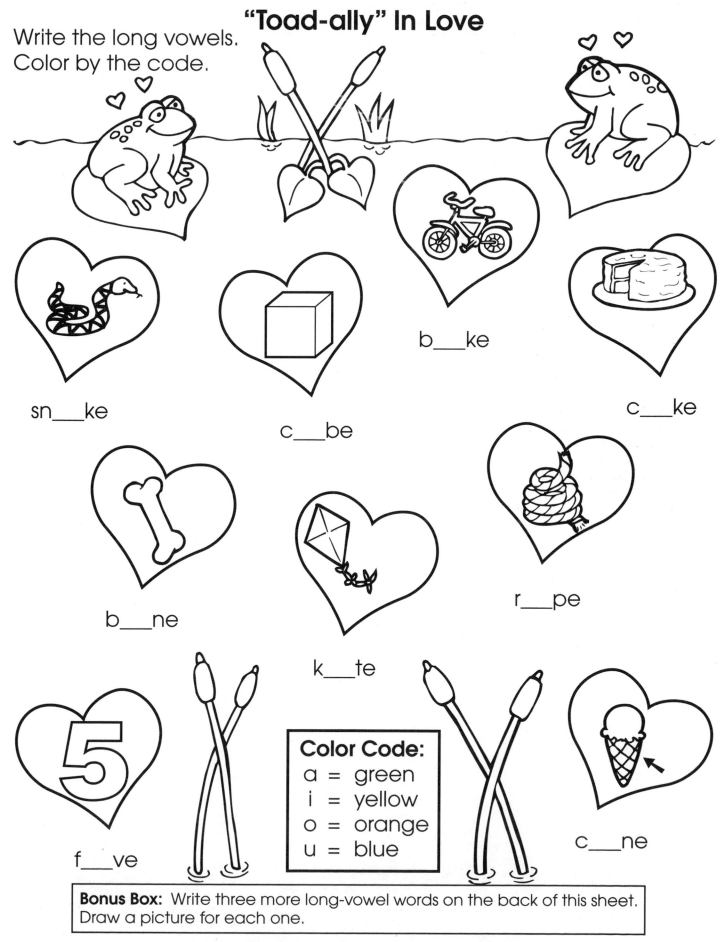

sn___ke

c___be

b___ke

c___ke

b___ne

k___te

r___pe

f___ve

Color Code:
a = green
i = yellow
o = orange
u = blue

c___ne

Bonus Box: Write three more long-vowel words on the back of this sheet.
Draw a picture for each one.

A Work Of Heart

Read each word.
Cut and paste to match.

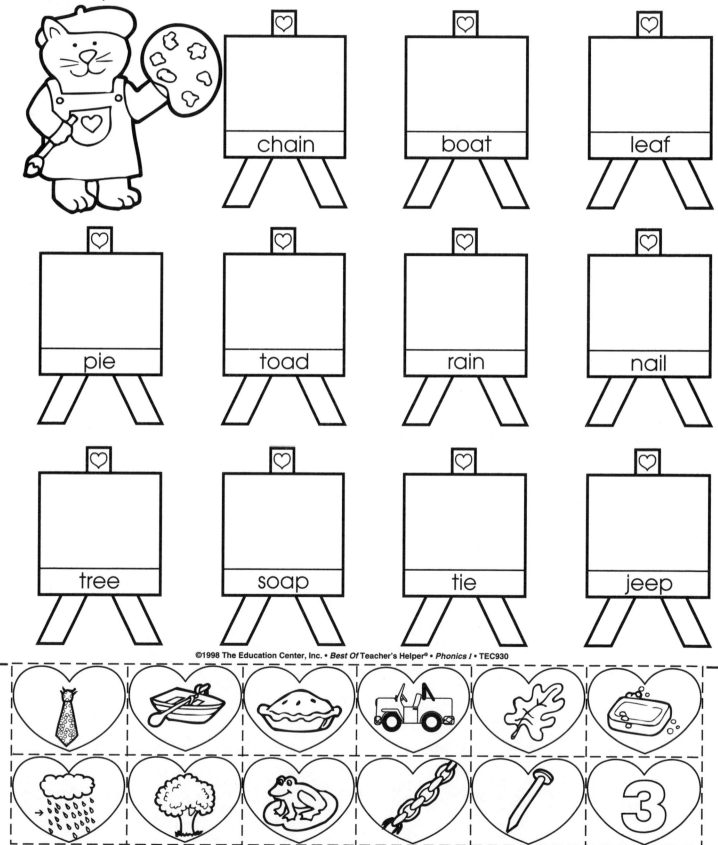

chain

boat

leaf

pie

toad

rain

nail

tree

soap

tie

jeep

©1998 The Education Center, Inc. • *Best Of* Teacher's Helper® • *Phonics I* • TEC930

Shamrock Harvest

Write the missing vowel. Each time you use a letter, cross it out on a shamrock.

r____pe

wh____le

k____y

tr____e

k____te

gh____st

sn____ke

c____at

s____al

a e o a i e o
  e   o   e   o

Penguin's Choice

Write each **long-vowel** word.
Read the word and find a picture
  to match.
Cut.
Glue.

Remember:
If you add a silent e,
the vowel
becomes long!

1. kit + e = _____

2. can + e = _____

3. tap + e = _____

4. not + e = _____

5. cub + e = _____

6. plan + e = _____

7. dim + e = _____

Farm Friends

Color each picture that has the **long-vowel** sound.

Dinosaur Hatchlings

Read the words.
Write the **long-vowel** words.

bell
beet
_ _ _ _ _ _ _

hope
hop
_ _ _ _ _ _ _

week
well
_ _ _ _ _ _ _

tap
tape
_ _ _ _ _ _ _

cute
cut
_ _ _ _ _ _ _

mill
mile
_ _ _ _ _ _ _

rope
rock
_ _ _ _ _ _ _

cup
cube
_ _ _ _ _ _ _

back
bake
_ _ _ _ _ _ _

like
lick
_ _ _ _ _ _ _

Bonus Box: On the back of this page, draw three dinosaur hatchlings.
Write a long-vowel name for each one. Color the dinosaurs.

Rain Makes The Tulips Grow

Read the words.
Write the **long-vowel** words.

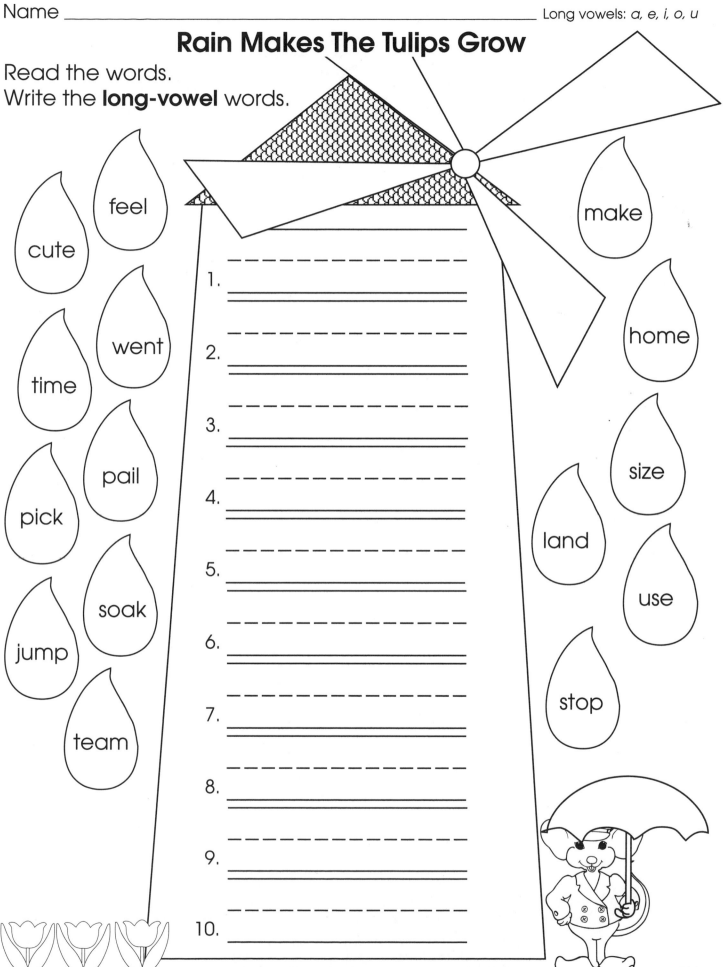

feel

cute

went

time

pail

pick

soak

jump

team

make

home

size

land

use

stop

1. _____

2. _____

3. _____

4. _____

5. _____

6. _____

7. _____

8. _____

9. _____

10. _____

Dinosaurs Find The Long-Vowel Words

Read the sentences.
Write the **long-vowel** words.

_____

- - - - - - - - - - - - - - - -

1. The mule sat down. _____

- - - - - - - - - - - - - - - -

2. The cat will chase that ball. _____

- - - - - - - - - - - - - - - -

3. Do you need a hat? _____

- - - - - - - - - - - - - - - -

4. Bob's wife went out. _____

- - - - - - - - - - - - - - - -

5. That joke is not funny. _____

- - - - - - - - - - - - - - - -

6. The house is for sale. _____

- - - - - - - - - - - - - - - -

7. Did you meet his mother? _____

- - - - - - - - - - - - - -

8. What time is the class? _____

- - - - - - - - - - - - - -

9. The dog hid the bone. _____

- - - - - - - - - - - - - -

10. Sam got a red tube. _____

Name _____

Dinosaur Decides

Name each picture.
Circle the vowel sound.

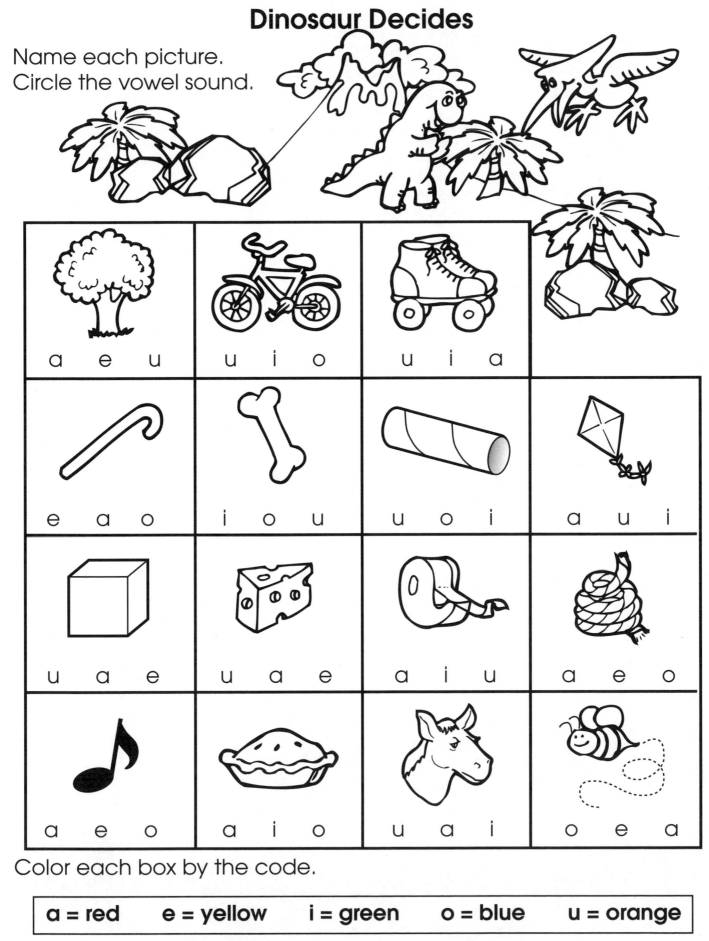

a e u	u i o	u i a	
e a o	i o u	u o i	a u i
u a e	u a e	a i u	a e o
a e o	a i o	u a i	o e a

Color each box by the code.

a = red	e = yellow	i = green	o = blue	u = orange

Name _____

Valentine Mail

Cut out and deliver the cards.
Glue **short a** words under box 1.
Glue **long a** words under box 2.

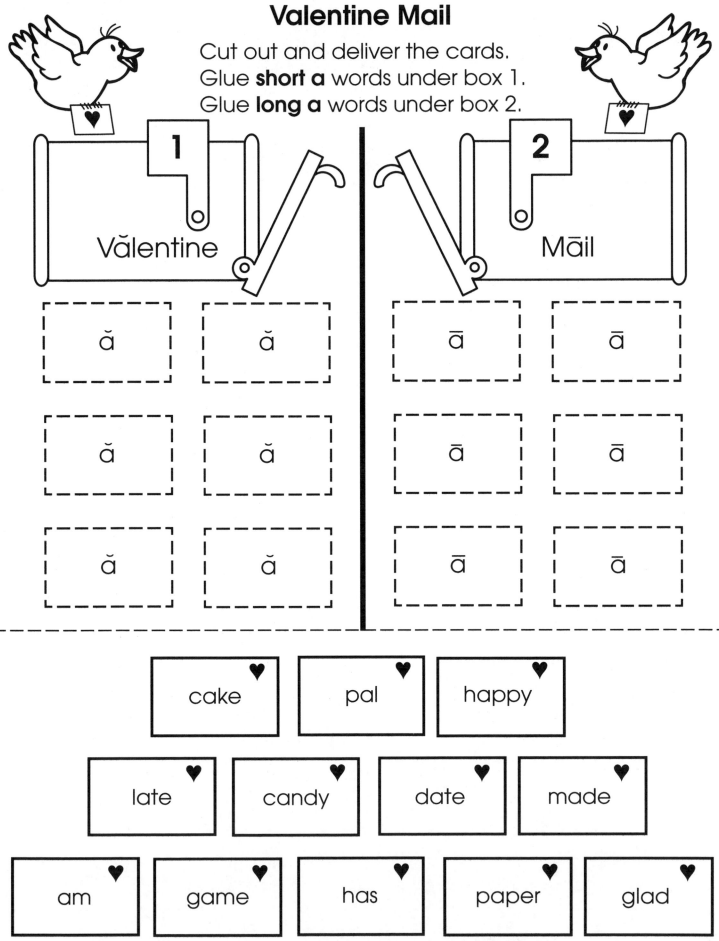

1	2
Vălentine	Māil

ă	ă	ā	ā
ă	ă	ā	ā
ă	ă	ā	ā

| cake | pal | happy |

| late | candy | date | made |

| am | game | has | paper | glad |

Sweet As Honey

Color the honey pots with **long a** words brown.
Color those with **short a** words green.
Write the words in the correct column.

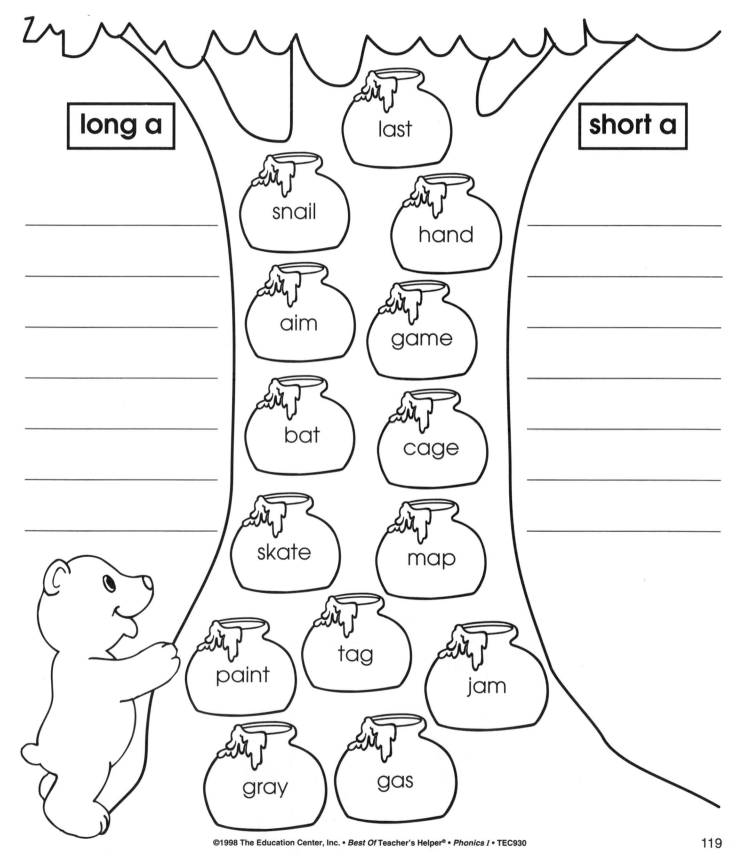

long a

short a

last

snail

hand

aim

game

bat

cage

skate

map

paint

tag

jam

gray

gas

Background For The Teacher

January 18 is the anniversary of the birth of A(lan) A(lexander) Milne, the English author especially remembered for the stories *Winnie-the-Pooh* (1926) and *The House at Pooh Corner* (1928).

Extension Activities

—Accompany Pooh Day with a honey-tasting day at school.

—Create your own classroom honey pots, and have children match fact Poohs to answers on honey pots, groups of coins to amounts on honey pots, etc.

—Use coloring books to make Winnie the Pooh and friends into stick puppets. Put them at a puppet center for creative interaction.

Answer Key

long a	short a
snail	last
game	hand
aim	bat
cage	map
paint	tag
skate	jam
gray	gas

Dental Duty

Write the ē words on Leo.
Write the ĕ words on Mr. Dentist.

Short ĕ

Long ē

seal   nest   bed   leaf   cheese
bee   tree   tent   net   bell

Background For The Teacher

The American Dental Association sponsors National Children's Dental Health Month each year in February. The month focuses on preventive dental health education. Children and adults are encouraged to take proper care of their teeth to prevent tooth and gum disease.

Extension Activities

— Children in the process of losing baby teeth will enjoy writing their names and the dates on large, cut-out paper teeth.

— Plan a class visit to a dentist's office, or invite a dentist to visit the class to demonstrate proper brushing and flossing. Write a thank-you note.

— Have children draw posters illustrating good dental health rules. Display these in the hall during Dental Health Month.

— To encourage dental health, create a "Smile!" bulletin board with photos of your students.

— Make a chart to help children keep track of how many times they brush in one week, or create a graph showing favorite toothpaste choices for a math activity.

Variation

Program the worksheet with words that have other vowel sounds. Change the directions before duplicating.

Answer Key

long ē	short ĕ
seal	nest
bee	bed
tree	tent
leaf	net
cheese	bell

Name _____

Vowel-Sound Touchdowns

Color the **long i** helmets red. Color the **short i** helmets blue.
Write the words under the correct goalposts.

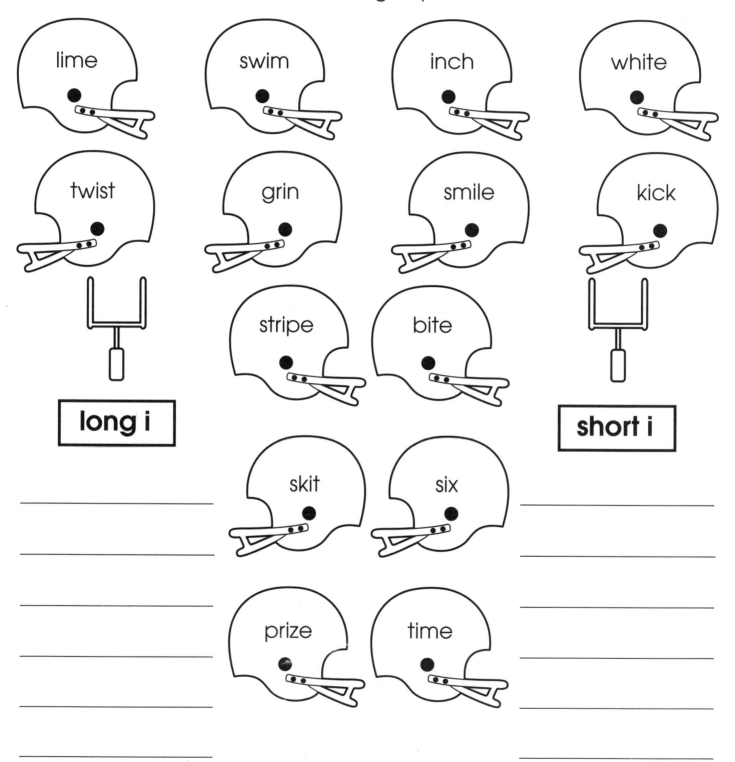

lime   swim   inch   white

twist   grin   smile   kick

stripe   bite

long i   **short i**

skit   six

prize   time

Name _____

Berry Christmas!

Color only **long i** berries. Color the wreath.
Cut out and glue on **long i** berries.

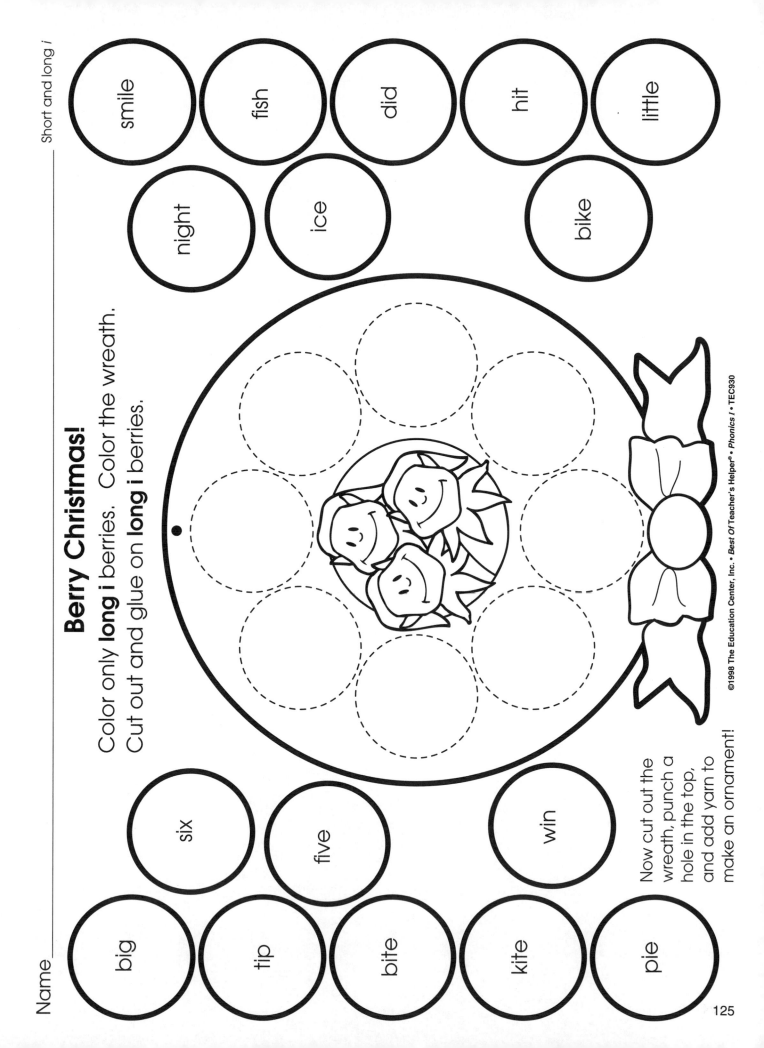

smile

fish

did

hit

little

night

ice

bike

six

five

win

big

tip

bite

kite

pie

Now cut out the
wreath, punch a
hole in the top,
and add yarn to
make an ornament!

Pots Of Vowels

Read the word on each tulip. Cut out and paste the word onto the correct pot.

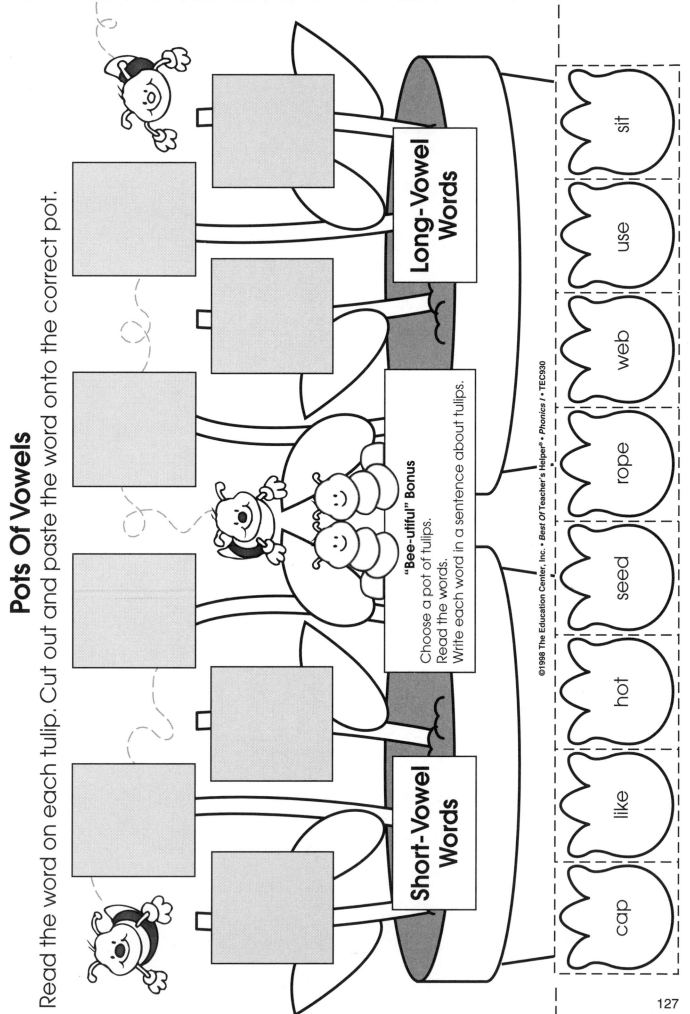

Long-Vowel Words

Short-Vowel Words

"Bee-utiful" Bonus

Choose a pot of tulips.
Read the words.
Write each word in a sentence about tulips.

sit

use

web

rope

seed

hot

like

cap

Name _____

Fish-Tank Phonics

Circle the word your teacher says.

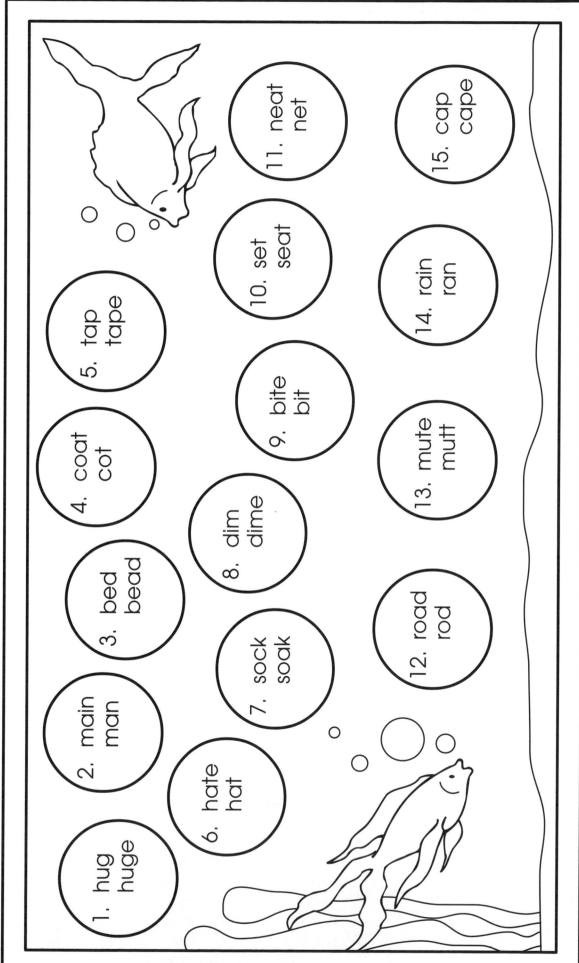

1. hug
huge

2. main
man

3. bed
bead

4. coat
cot

5. tap
tape

6. hate
hat

7. sock
soak

8. dim
dime

9. bite
bit

10. set
seat

11. neat
net

12. road
rod

13. mute
mutt

14. rain
ran

15. cap
cape

Oral Instructions For Page 129

1. Circle the word **hug** in number one.
2. Circle the word **man** in number two.
3. Circle the word **bed** in number three.
4. Circle the word **cot** in number four.
5. Circle the word **tape** in number five.
6. Circle the word **hate** in number six.
7. Circle the word **soak** in number seven.
8. Circle the word **dim** in number eight.
9. Circle the word **bite** in number nine.
10. Circle the word **seat** in number ten.
11. Circle the word **neat** in number eleven.
12. Circle the word **rod** in number twelve.
13. Circle the word **mute** in number thirteen.
14. Circle the word **rain** in number fourteen.
15. Circle the word **cape** in number fifteen.

Variations

— Mask the words in each bubble and the directions. Have students write answers for math tests in the bubbles.

— Mask the words in each bubble and the directions. Add new directions and fill the bubbles with:
  — assignments to be completed
  — words to study
  — math facts to practice

— Mask the words in each bubble and the directions. Add new directions and reprogram with:
  — color words for coloring
  — math problems to solve
  — two words to be made into contractions
  — numbers in sequence with one number missing

Answer Key

1. hug	8. dim
2. man	9. bite
3. bed	10. seat
4. cot	11. neat
5. tape	12. rod
6. hate	13. mute
7. soak	14. rain
	15. cape

Name _____

Springtime In The Rockies

Color Code: long a = blue
short a = red
long e = yellow
short e = green
short u = purple

tent

grass

snake

whale

skunk

tree

bee

cheese

grape

nest

drum

flag

duck

crab

Background For The Teacher

Spring is signaled by blossoming fruit trees, flowers, and flowering shrubs. Among the first flowers to poke their heads through the snow are the daffodils, crocuses, and tulips. Many areas of the country have spring flower festivals, such as the Dogwood Festival in Atlanta, Georgia, the Cherry Blossom Festival in San Francisco, California, and the Tulip Time Festival in Pella, Iowa.

Extension Activities

— Use colored tissue paper to create azalea, cherry, apple, or forsythia blossoms. Pinch small tissue squares into blossoms and glue along a branch. Anchor branches in a flowerpot with clay or stones.

— Have children cut and paste magazine pictures of flowers for a colorful collage. Display pictures of flowers and compare.

— Study the parts of a flower. Obtain one flower for each child from flowers discarded by florists. Provide a magnifying glass for a closer examination.

— Examine flower seeds, and read packet instructions to children. Plant several kinds in labeled containers. Record growth on a calendar. Have each child take a seedling home to transplant. Marigolds are a quick flowering, hardy variety.

— Force a bulb to bloom. Bring in bulbs that have been buried for 10–12 weeks. Place in a cool, dark place. Keep watered. When sprouts are four inches high, place in light occasionally.

— Display gardening equipment and tools. Explain their uses, and list related vocabulary.

— Discover how seeds sprout by placing radish seeds between a dampened paper towel and the inside of a glass jar. Cover jar. Keep paper damp and watch seeds germinate.

Answer Key

Name

A Wagon Full Of Wishes

Use the code to color the hearts.

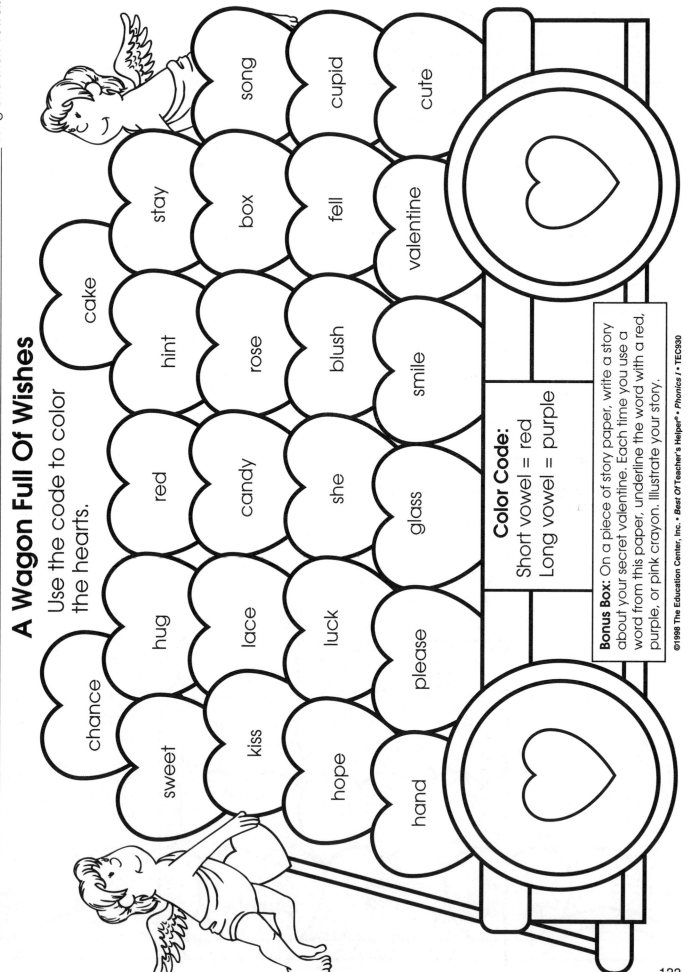

Color Code:
Short vowel = red
Long vowel = purple

Bonus Box: On a piece of story paper, write a story about your secret valentine. Each time you use a word from this paper, underline the word with a red, purple, or pink crayon. Illustrate your story.

Hearts contain the words: song, cupid, cute, stay, box, fell, valentine, cake, hint, rose, blush, smile, red, candy, she, glass, hug, lace, luck, please, chance, sweet, kiss, hope, hand

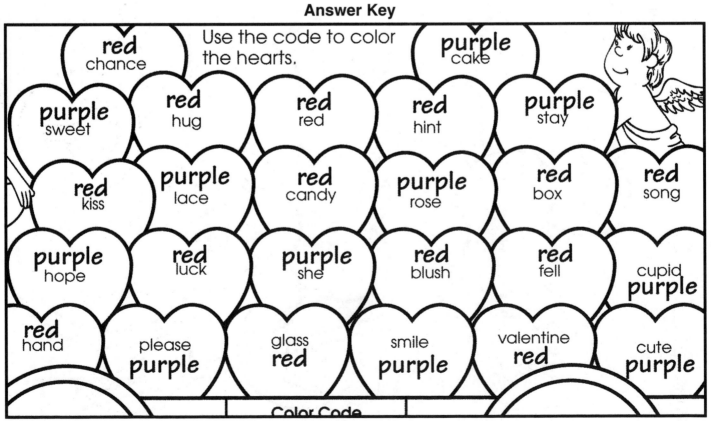

Use the code to color the hearts.

red
chance

purple
cake

purple
sweet

red
hug

red
red

red
hint

purple
stay

red
kiss

purple
lace

red
candy

purple
rose

red
box

red
song

purple
hope

red
luck

purple
she

red
blush

red
fell

cupid
purple

red
hand

please
purple

glass
red

smile
purple

valentine
red

cute
purple

Color Code

134

Bonnets And Bunnies

Draw bunny ears on the **short-vowel** circles.
Draw a bonnet on the **long-vowel** circles.

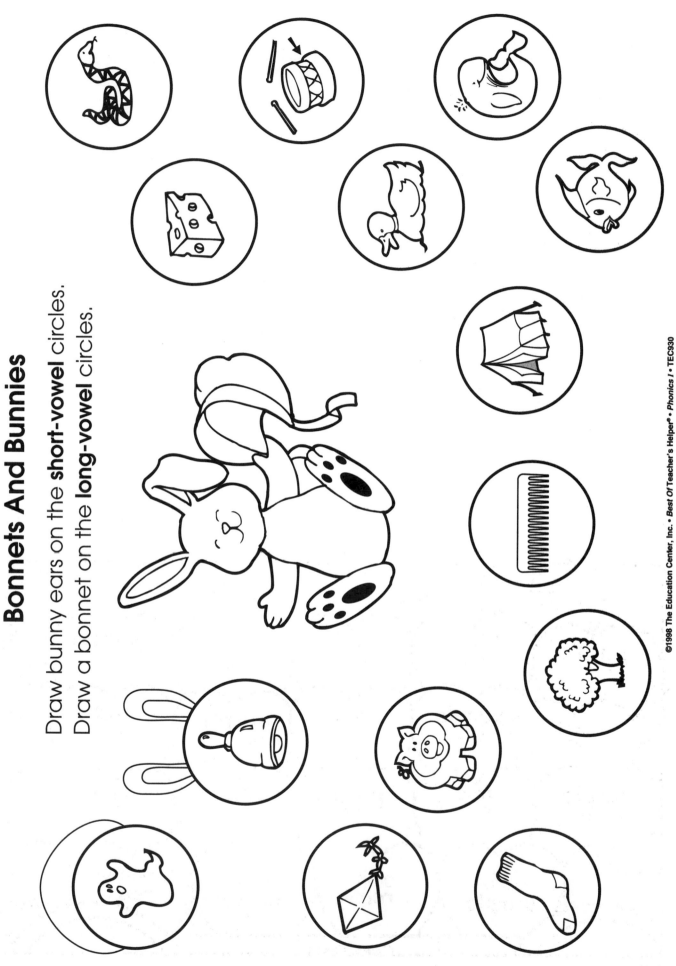

Name _____

Ducky Duet

Each raindrop has a picture of a **long o** or **short o** word. Cut out the raindrops.
Paste each one on the correct umbrella.

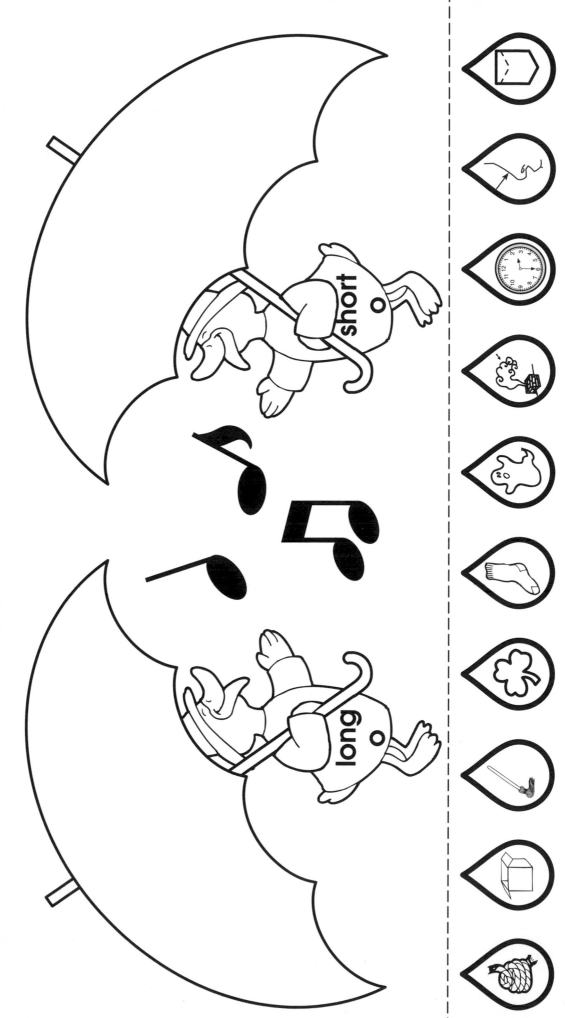

long

short

Name _____

Sunshine For Groundhog Day

Help Mr. Groundhog draw suns around word pairs with the same vowel sound.

cat
pan

cake
aim

pack
late

queen
team

peek
net

red
pens

gate
stay

king
milk

tin
line

light
sing

green
beads

prize
mile

leg
bell

meat
left

Background For The Teacher

According to an old superstition, the groundhog leaves its burrow on February 2, Groundhog Day. If it sees its shadow, it returns underground for six weeks, and there are six more weeks of winter.

A groundhog, also called a woodchuck, is a large rodent found in open woods and ravines in most of Canada and the northeastern United States. It is heavyset and covered with thick, brownish hair. Green vegetation is the groundhog's diet. It nests and hibernates in winter in its burrow of many compartments.

Black-Cat Cookies

Draw cookies around the **br** pictures. Color the cat black.

Name _____

Defensive Blends

Fill in the missing blends.
Write the words under the football player.

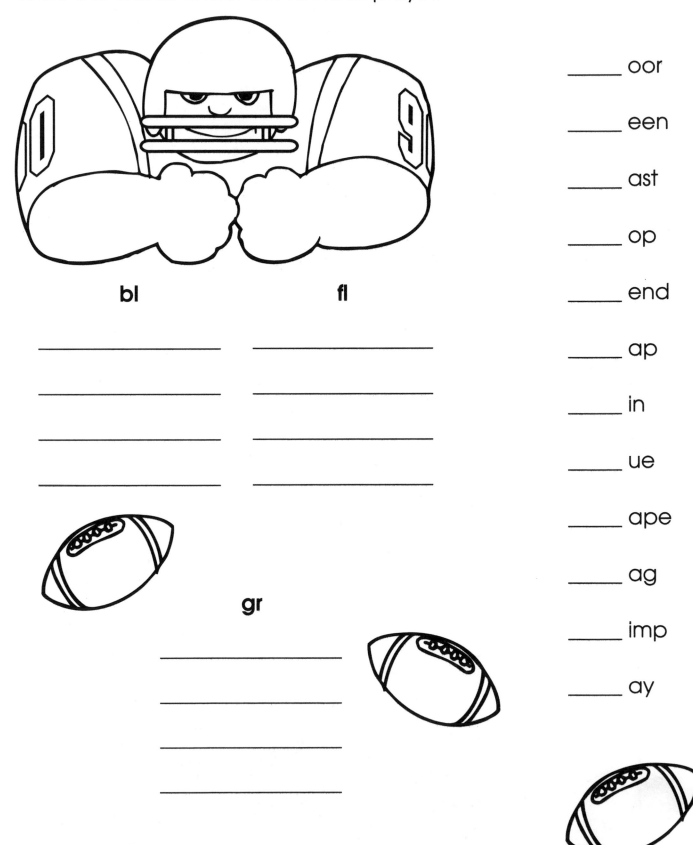

bl

fl

gr

____ oor

____ een

____ ast

____ op

____ end

____ ap

____ in

____ ue

____ ape

____ ag

____ imp

____ ay

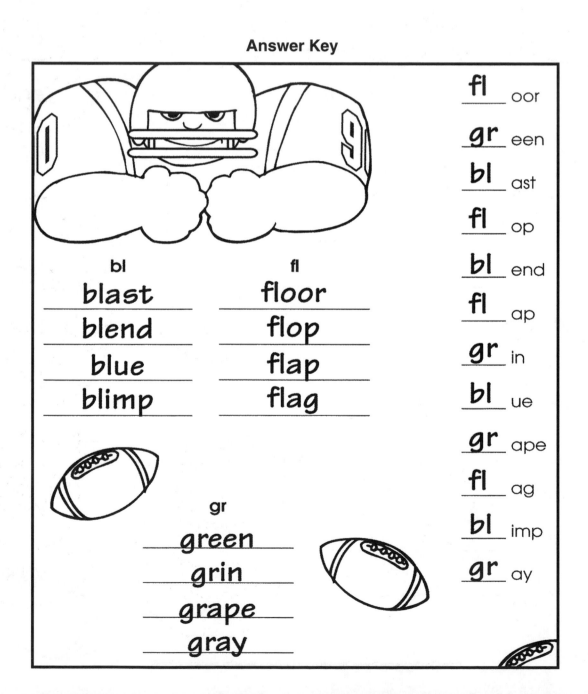

bl

blast
blend
blue
blimp

fl

floor
flop
flap
flag

gr

green
grin
grape
gray

fl_ oor

gr_ een

bl_ ast

fl_ op

bl_ end

fl_ ap

gr_ in

bl_ ue

gr_ ape

fl_ ag

bl_ imp

gr_ ay

Name _____

Blooming Blends

Say the name for each picture.
Listen for the beginning blend.
Color by the code.

Color Code:
cr = yellow
dr = orange
fr = pink
gr = green

Variation

Mask directions. Write new ones for ending sounds or for vowel sounds.

Answer Key

Blends: *fl, fr, gl, pl, sl*

Wheelbarrow Blends

Cut and paste to match the blends.

fr	pl	sl	gl	fl
fr	pl	sl	gl	fl

Bonus Box:
Pretend that you looked around the barnyard and found the things shown above. On the back of this page, write about how the farmer could use three of them.

Name _____

Churning Out Blends

Cut and paste to match the blends.

sp	sk	st	sm	sn	**Bonus Box:**
sp	sk	st	sm	sn	Write about something that happened on a farm. Use three or more of the picture words from above.

Name _____

Cotton's "Cat-astrophes"

Use your pencil to fill in the circle beside the correct word.

1. Cotton is my cat. He looks like a soft, white ball of _____.
   ○ fluff   ○ gruff

2. When Cotton stands in _____, you only see his face.
   ○ snow   ○ slow

3. Don't leave Cotton in the snow too long. He might _____.
   ○ breeze   ○ freeze

4. The little girl who lives next door says he's as white as a _____.
   ○ proud   ○ cloud

5. Cotton loves to play with a ball of _____.
   ○ string   ○ sting

6. He'll get down low and _____ his tail.
   ○ snitch   ○ twitch

7. Cotton sometimes leaps into the air as if he's going to _____.
   ○ fry   ○ fly

8. He'll bat a ball of string around the floor and watch it _____.
   ○ spin   ○ twin

9. As he runs after the ball, he will sometimes _____ into things.
   ○ trash   ○ smash

10. One day Cotton made the milk _____ from his bowl.
    ○ skill   ○ spill

11. One time when Cotton was playing, he _____ a flower vase.
    ○ smoke   ○ broke

12. But Cotton didn't mean to make a mess. He is a _____ cat.
    ○ sleet   ○ sweet

Bonus Box: Read the sentences again. Choose one. Draw a picture showing what the sentence is about.

Variations

— Have students write each sentence on handwriting paper after filling in the circles.

— Have advanced students write some of the sentences to form a paragraph about Cotton. Have students illustrate their paragraphs.

Answer Key

1. Cotton is my cat. He looks like a soft, white ball of _____.
   - ● fluff
   - ○ gruff

2. When Cotton stands in _____, you only see his face.
   - ● snow
   - ○ slow

3. Don't leave Cotton in the snow too long. He might _____.
   - ○ breeze
   - ● freeze

4. The little girl who lives next door says he's as white as a _____.
   - ○ proud
   - ● cloud

5. Cotton loves to play with a ball of _____.
   - ● string
   - ○ sting

6. He'll get down low and _____ his tail.
   - ○ snitch
   - ● twitch

7. Cotton sometimes leaps into the air as if he's going to _____.
   - ○ fry
   - ● fly

8. He'll bat a ball of string around the floor and watch it _____.
   - ● spin
   - ○ twin

9. As he runs after the ball, he will sometimes _____ into things.
   - ○ trash
   - ● smash

10. One day Cotton made the milk _____ from his bowl.
    - ○ skill
    - ● spill

11. One time when Cotton was playing, he _____ a flower vase.
    - ○ smoke
    - ● broke

12. But Cotton didn't mean to make a mess. He is a _____ cat.
    - ○ sleet
    - ● sweet

Name _____ Blends, digraphs

Bobby Bookworm

Find out what Bobby is reading about.
Draw a book around the picture in each box that matches the
   beginning sound.

©1998 The Education Center, Inc. • *Best Of* Teacher's Helper® • *Phonics I* • TEC930

153

Answer Key

Ice-Skate Blends

Fill in the missing letters.

cl   pl   ch   mp

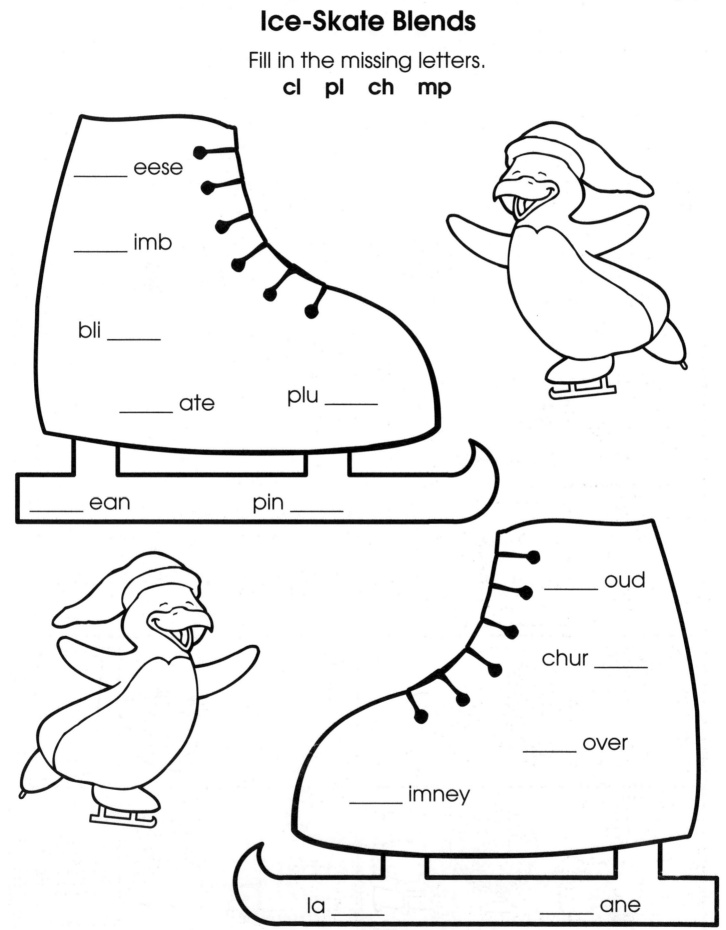

____ eese

____ imb

bli ____

____ ate   plu ____

____ ean   pin ____

____ oud

chur ____

____ over

____ imney

la ____   ____ ane

Bug Bodies

Fold a sheet of paper into thirds.
Paste a head at the top of each section.
Paste body parts under heads by **ch**, **th** and **sh** sounds.
Add legs to make "bugs."

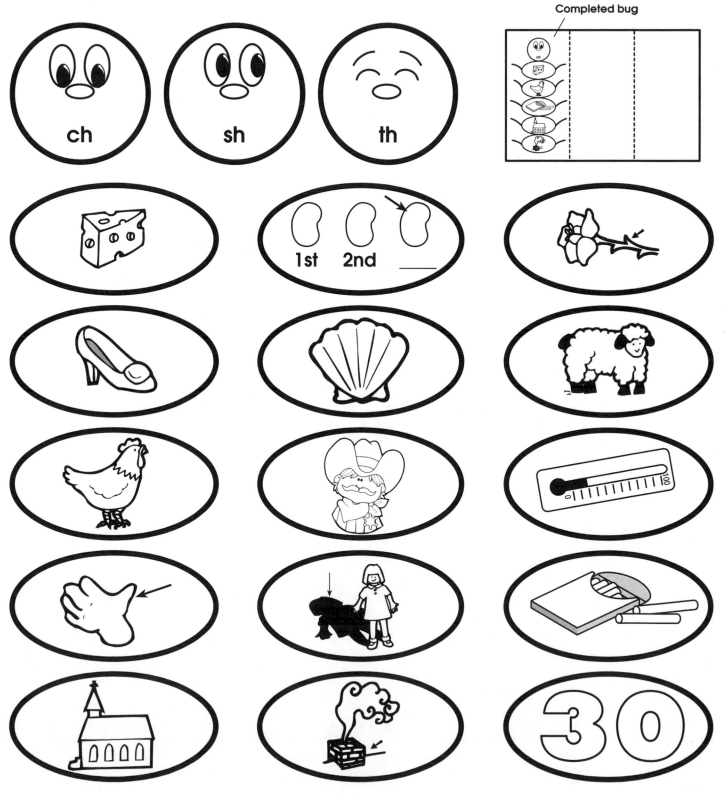